SIDE ADVENTURE

SIDE ADVENTURE

THE PLAYBOOK TO LEVERAGE YOUR
CORPORATE JOB, PURSUE A SIDE VENTURE,
AND FIND HAPPINESS AND FULFILLMENT.

Artin Nazarian

gatekeeper press™

Columbus, Ohio

The views and opinions expressed in this book are solely those of the author and do not reflect the views or opinions of Gatekeeper Press. Gatekeeper Press is not to be held responsible for and expressly disclaims responsibility of the content herein.

Side Adventure: The playbook to leverage your corporate job, pursue a side venture, and find happiness and fulfillment.

Book cover concept by Violeta Loana State

Published by Gatekeeper Press

2167 Stringtown Rd, Suite 109

Columbus, OH 43123-2989

www.GatekeeperPress.com

Library of Congress Control Number: 2020949181

ISBN (hardcover): 9781662906220

ISBN (paperback): 9781662906237

eISBN: 9781662906244

Table of Contents

DEDICATION

This book is dedicated to my wife Alice, my son Eric, my daughter Ava, my parents, sister, and everyone else who has been part of my journey, challenging me to get better along the way.

Alice, thank you for your undying support, allowing and encouraging me to pursue this book and side ventures and making me realize the importance of family. You are the glue that keeps it all together.

Eric, you have taught me so much in less than two years. Thank you for bringing so much joy into our life. I know one day you will stop saying "hi dada" so I'm going to cherish every moment before you grow up.

Mom, Dad, and Anita, you have become the best grandparents and aunt a grandson can ask for. I can see how much Eric loves you. We appreciate you helping us with all the hours babysitting. You have been supporting me my entire life, and without your help, this book would have been difficult to pursue.

Baby Ava, thank you for allowing me to be a Girl Dad. I can't wait to tell you about all the things that happened in the year you were born. Hopefully you will give me a couple of extra years of "hi dada."

Brian, I am deeply indebted to you. A lot of this would not be possible without you, and I consider myself fortunate to be able to call you a friend.

Barrie, you have been a coach and mentor to me for over fifteen years. I have learned a lot from you, which has helped me become a better leader.

Michael, thank you for your incredible friendship and partnership.

Thank you to everyone who read the manuscript and helped me make it better.

Thank you for purchasing Side Adventure.

For bonus material only for insiders,
please visit the below URL.

www.bonus.sideadventure.com

CHAPTER 1

INTRODUCTION

"The most important thing is to try and inspire people so that they can be great in whatever they want to do."
Kobe Bryant

We all strive to land that dream job or have our own company that makes us feel like we'll never work a day in our life because we love what we do so much. Isn't that what Steve Jobs, Bill Gates, Mark Zuckerberg, Jeff Bezos, and others like them did? Although this might be true to some extent, it is not 100 percent true.

In most cases, you did not know what you were passionate about in your early twenties, and if you did, you have since realized you had not dug deep enough to understand who you are as a person and what you're truly passionate about. To find ourselves, we go through the education system, taking classes that seem irrelevant and hoping that things will work themselves out after graduation—shouldn't an education equal success? Graduation happens and you can no longer hide behind the curtain of "I'm a student." Now you have to become a contributing member of society. You already have student debt, so continuing schooling for an MBA or any post-graduate degree doesn't seem appealing, but some of us do it anyway assuming that is where you will find the answers and live happily ever after.

Since most of us don't come from a family that is well-off and can support us, real-world adult needs force us to get a job so we can pay the bills. If you got a job at a small company or startup, you soon realize you are working long hours, going above and beyond in the hopes of earning that big paycheck when the company is acquired. If you got a job at a large company, you realize how much politics exist between different departments and people, and you spend a good chunk of your time just navigating these politics instead of doing work. And after all of your contributions, you are told you just have to be patient if you want a promotion. This is the message Baby Boomers want to convey to the younger generations because patience worked for them. But that just doesn't work for us. Times have changed.

After getting settled into your job, you might feel less financial stress. However, a few years go by and you ask yourself: What happened to the dream I had? Do I even care about my current job? Where did my creativity go? You daydream about quitting your job and telling your boss that, if they had just given you a chance, you would have been able to drive the company to real success. But then, the daydream ends, and with shoulders down you go back to your work. You have a great idea but have no idea where to start. You are not an engineer. You did not graduate from Stanford, Harvard, or MIT. You don't have a network that can guide you. You do some research online, but generic information is not that useful for someone in your position. Now what? Do you just settle?

I have been through all of this, and I want to tell you that you should NEVER settle. I felt frustrated that even though I was climbing the corporate ladder, it was slow and not equal to the value I was adding. I had options to jump to another company, but I knew it wouldn't have been any different. My hunger and drive were much bigger than most companies could handle. So, I had only one solution. What drove me—and what still drives me—was the idea that I didn't want to live this life as a number, but as someone who had a positive impact and left a legacy. I knew I had to figure out how to bring my software ideas to life without having any experience in coding or design. I barely knew how to use photoshop, but I was resourceful and willing to learn. I knew that when I put my mind on something, there was nothing I couldn't figure out. I also knew that if I failed, it would still be a great learning experience, which would help me with my next idea. As long as I was in pursuit of my goals and dreams, I wouldn't let frustrations at my job bother me. I knew, with conviction, that I was one idea away from happiness.

Well, I failed multiple times, but I was energized. It took me many years to succeed. There is a lot that goes into bringing an idea to life and then convincing others to buy into it. This is why I am writing this book. I want to share with you what I learned the hard way and how I excelled in the corporate world, got promoted multiple times, made more money while leveraging my job to pursue my software product ideas, got an education better than any MBA without the debt, raised $4 million, launched a hospitality software company, and discovered what my passion is and how I want to give back. I'm not talking about some generic, high-level five-step process. I want to give you practical information that you can use to create your own action plan. I want to help you have a much smaller learning curve than I did.

I have been helping out others in my circle, giving speeches to organizations and universities, but I want to reach even more people that might benefit from my failures, experiences, and successes. The long journey also helped me figure out what happiness means to me, and I want to help you figure this out faster than I did so you have more time in your life to go pursue it. You are also one idea away from happiness as you define it.

The book is titled *Side Adventure* because pursuing a side venture is truly an adventure. It has taken me to many cities in the United States, including but not limited to New York, Miami,

Chicago, Austin, and San Francisco. It has allowed me to travel outside of the United States to the South of France, Amsterdam, Paris, and Barcelona, to name a few. I have met incredible people along the way—investors, entrepreneurs, celebrities. I attended a very memorable product launch party that included Kanye West and Skrillex as our headlining performers.

Of course, there were many failures, but failures are learning experiences, and successes are a platform to pay it forward. Let the adventure begin!

CHAPTER 2

MY STORY

"If you're afraid to fail, then you're
probably going to fail."
Kobe Bryant

I was born in Tehran, Iran in 1977 during a turmoil period, which was compounded by the fact that we were Christians living in a Muslim country. I had just turned two when the revolution happened, the Shah was forced out, and Khomeini and his Islamic regime took over. Shortly after, the decade-long Iran-Iraq war began.

Most of you will probably remember back to Desert Storm and what that war looked like through the lens of the media. It was nothing like that. There were no strategic targets and laser guide bombs. The Iraqi planes would fly over the city and drop bombs in residential areas. It had become so common that as soon as we heard the sound of an object whistling in the sky, we knew a flash of light would follow soon, the sound of the blast a few seconds after. Every window was taped with an X shape to reduce glass shattering as a result of the sound waves. When the government alarms went off, people would go on their roofs to watch the anti-aircraft missiles as if it were a firework show. The day my family was trying to leave the country, a bomb attack delayed our departure. But we made it out eventually and moved to Spain, where my family and I lived as refugees.

For about a year, Madrid was our home. I was a carefree fourth-grader, and the fact that I did not speak a word of

Spanish did not bother me. The language barrier was short-lived as I quickly picked up Spanish and felt accepted in school. My earliest entrepreneurial venture started when I began drawing cartoon characters and selling them to other students. In a very short period of time, I started getting requests and pre-orders. My first official business was born. I fell in love with the country, the people, and the culture. To this day, Spain is the team I root for during the World Cup—even though 2014 and 2018 were not good years.

During that year in Madrid, we visited some of the other cities in Spain, including Toledo, Segovia, and Barcelona. That is when the travel bug was inserted into my head. I loved traveling and visiting new cities, experiencing and learning about new cultures and their history, especially if the history spans back thousands of years. Roman history fascinated me at a very young age. I could not wrap my head around the fact that over two thousand years ago, the Aqueduct in Segovia, the castle in Toledo, and the entire gothic quarter in Barcelona was built without any of the modern tools and computers available to us today. Strangely, it gave me confidence that if ancient Romans could build cities and castles thousands of years ago, then I would be able to innovate whatever I wanted. This confidence and positive outlook have been engraved in my head ever since.

It was toward the end of 1988 when my family was awarded Green Cards to enter the United States. Our journey moved us from Madrid to Glendale, California, a city quite different from Madrid. Glendale was a suburb at that time and had a history of less than 100 years. Many Armenian refugees had been moving to Glendale during the 1980s, so it felt more like home for my parents, as we had some family already there who were able to show us the ropes and guide us through our new American life. But why did so many Armenians choose Glendale? I wondered.

Being interested in history, I did some research and I found that the earliest record of Armenians in the United States dated back to the Colonial period, but it wasn't until the late nineteenth century and early twentieth century that Armenians started immigrating to the East Coast of the United States amongst the wave of immigrants from other countries around the same period. This was mainly driven by the Young Turks movement, which led to the Armenian Genocide and a further disbursement of Armenians to various countries in that region. Some of the Armenians who were living in Boston, New York, and New Jersey had farming experience and they moved west to central California—most notably Fresno—to be part of the booming farming industry. It wasn't until the 1950s and 1960s that a large number of Armenian families migrated to Southern California, and by the mid-1970s, there were Armenian churches and schools established. Prominent Armenians with political and business influence were already living in Glendale, which inspired other Armenians to move to the town as well. Meanwhile, several global events were taking place—the Iranian Revolution, the Iran-Iraq War, the Lebanese Civil War, the collapse of the Soviet Union, and the economic crash of Armenia in the 1990s—which lead to Armenian refugees migrating to the United States to set roots in Glendale and neighboring cities.

And that's why we moved from Madrid to Glendale. I ended up going to elementary school, middle school, and high school in Glendale. In elementary school, I would volunteer as a translator since I could speak Armenian, Spanish, English, and Farsi.

Within the first year of living in Glendale, I was exposed to basketball and the Showtime Lakers, and my love for basketball and all sports was instantly seeded. I was drawn to anything that had a ball. Only bad weather could get me off the courts and fields. My friends and I would play basketball and baseball until the sun went down and we could not see the ball. At twelve years old, there was nothing I wanted more than to become a professional athlete. I was playing in organized leagues, and I was really good compared to other kids.

Once I got to high school, reality kicked in. I played against kids that were significantly taller and better. I was not going to be 6'6" and 230lbs before I went to college. I knew that being a pro athlete in one of the four major sports was not in my future, but I loved sports so much I continued to learn about pro sports.

This had a big impact on my life. I learned the importance of teamwork by studying great coaches. I learned leadership lessons, which I then applied to my corporate job and startups. Every team I have had the privilege to lead knows that I hate the word *boss*. Instead, I want to be known as *Coach,* and just like how Michael Jordan and Kobe Bryant needed a great coach to perform at their best, a business team also has stars and role players that need a coach to help them perform at their best.

Living in Los Angeles, I was also heavily exposed to the film industry. I would watch the Oscars and visualize myself on that stage. I was drawn to the glitz and glamour, and it took me a few more years to understand why I was drawn to the movies. From drawing characters in my pre-teen years, I transitioned to using camcorders and making music videos and short movies with my friends. This interest grew strong, and with the support of my parents, I decided to go to film school.

In my early years of college, when taking my general education classes, I worked at one of the major department stores selling women's shoes. It was at this job that I learned my next valuable lesson: the importance of customer service. I had not yet strengthened my sales skills at this age, but because of the importance I put in customer service, I was always one of the top performers. It was also at this job I met Michael. He had transferred to my department from another store around the time I was finishing my general education classes and we soon realized we were about to attend the same film school. A bond was formed instantly—one that is still burning hot to this date—and we have helped and challenged each other for the last twenty years.

Once I started my film studies and making short student films, I realized that wanting to be in the film industry because of the glitz and glamour was not a good reason. I was young and not mature enough to know that wanting to do something because of external factors doesn't usually equate to success. I realized that the reason I was attracted to making movies was because I was attracted to creating and building. I wanted to take an idea that was in my head and share it with everyone else. This was a big realization for me. I had the entrepreneurial itch.

In order to graduate from film school, every student had to either direct and produce their own short film or have a key role in another student's film. The school also offered grants to a limited number of projects. You would submit your short script and proposal and they would select five projects to offer $5,000 grants to. I was fortunate that my project was one of the five chosen, and the $5,000 grant covered half of my budget. As a student with immigrant parents who were barely making it financially, I was broke. As a kid, I remember playing basketball with denim shorts instead of basketball shorts and saving $1.07 to buy a Whopper from Burger King so I didn't have to burden my parents. And now I had to figure out how to raise another $5,000 on my own.

While brainstorming on how to raise $5,000, I thought about the market I had easy access to, other film students, and what they wanted. Although I had not yet learned the concept of identifying a problem, coming up with a solution, getting feedback, and executing, I can see that I instinctively followed these very steps. What did film students want? To become successful filmmakers. How could they get noticed? By creating their own short film and submitting them to various film festivals in the hope that it got accepted.

Students would submit to as many film festivals as they could, so I knew film festivals were not competing against each other. This is where I began doing competitor analysis, understanding the barrier to entry and learning about the customer. As a result, I launched my own film festival. Part of the requirements to graduate was to complete a semester as an intern. To complete this requirement, I got an internship at one of the major film studios helping a senior-level executive with administrative tasks. With this, I built a relationship with this executive and a few others. To give my film festival credibility, I got the executives to be judges for the film festival. This is where I pitched my idea to get resources, which in this scenario was executives' own time, before really understanding how professional pitches are done.

I created a simple website and placed posters all around campus, which prompted word-of-mouth marketing. Before I knew it, I had film festival entry checks delivered via mail to my parents' house. Once all the entries were in, finalists were chosen and screened at a theater where the studio executives chose a winner. The festival was a huge success and I delivered the value promised—another important concept in launching a product or business. The value returned to me was that I was able to raise about $4,000.

I was $1,000 short of my budget. This helped me with my next lesson. A movie is a product, and to manufacture any product you need suppliers and vendors. One lever an entrepreneur has to control is the cost of goods and vendor rates for services being rendered. You can always try to negotiate discounts, which is what I was doing. I ended up negotiating a discount from a production rental facility and I was ready to shoot my short film.

After a few months, my short film was complete. I was so proud of myself, even though it was an amateur piece of work. After all the students completed their projects, the film school held a showcase where they presented the seven or eight best short films in a big theater. Friends and family were invited. It felt like a big premier. I thought I was on my way to becoming a big shot Hollywood filmmaker.

Finally, it was time for my short film. Lights were dimmed and the credits began to roll. When my credits were on screen, "Written and Directed by Artin Nazarian," I looked to the left where my parents were sitting, and they had the biggest smile on their face. And that's when it hit me. I once wanted to be in the film industry because of the glitz and glamour, but in my early days of film school, I realized I was drawn to building and creating things that would allow me to leave a legacy.

At that moment, in the theater, I realized that even wanting to build and create had its purpose. I wanted to make my parents proud. They had been through so much and had sacrificed everything to move our family to a new country. I had just identified my internal purpose and what drove my core. I wanted to build and create to leave a legacy. That was my external purpose. My external purpose would help me fulfill my internal purpose. Seeing my parents proud would make me happy. Isn't happiness what everyone is after? I was twenty-two years old and I realized that everything we do is to feel happiness. It is the ultimate emotion we all strive for. I understood that to be happy I had to have a meaningful and positive purpose in life. A big weight was lifted off my shoulders, as being a successful filmmaker was no longer the only option. There were multiple routes to get to the emotion I was after.

About a month later, I graduated. My internship had already ended. I felt like an incredibly wise, yet extremely broke, twenty-two-year-old. I would use a payday advance service to pay for things, which only made my financial situation worse. I was not having any luck landing a decent job, and to make ends meet I went back to my job selling women's shoes. This was certainly not how I had pictured my immediate future after graduation.

What made things bearable was that Michael was still working in the same department. One weekend, as Michael and I were behind the cash registers, Michael's customer handed him a credit card. We recognized the card to be from the credit union of one of the major studios. We had a brief conversation with her and Michael got her email address. Weeks later, I was going in for an interview. Was this really happening? One minute I was selling women's shoes and the next I was interviewing at a major studio. I guess it's true that it's not *what* you know, but *who* you know. After my interview ended, I got in my car and drove off. Within five minutes, I got a call from HR and they offered me the position. I couldn't believe how easy it had been. Was I just well-prepared for the interview? I sure hoped so!

The job I had landed was in-home postproduction and distribution. Nothing that was taught in film school. I went from being broke for the last five years to now making $30,000 a year, which felt like a big number to me back then. I had racked up a huge debt and I was finally able to pay it off. Although the steady income afforded me a bit of freedom, I was not happy nor satisfied. And that's when it hit me: money doesn't buy happiness, but it does give you options. Options to do both smart and dumb things. Options to live a healthier life or the complete opposite. Options to surround yourself with people that lift you up or pull you down. How you use the additional options you have can lead to happiness, but money does not guarantee happiness.

I approached my job with an entrepreneurial mindset: How can I add more value for my customers than my competitors? This led to quick promotions. Within five or six years, I was officially considered a studio executive before I was thirty. But there were also many lows. Feeling underappreciated, bosses that lead by fear and created toxic cultures of "yes" people, bosses that were short-sighted and only favored a handful of people that resembled their own style, and draining corporate politics. I did not allow this to kill my entrepreneurial spirit. I used it as motivation.

During the first few years, Michael and I made various attempts at entrepreneurial ventures ranging from a commercial production company putting to use what we had learned in film school, to writing and developing websites. All failed for one reason or another, but were great learning experiences. With the dot com bubble and Web 2.0, using software to run a business smartly and efficiently became a must. As a result, I got involved in a lot of system development projects at my job, which, combined with failed website ventures, meant that I had gained a lot of valuable experience, insight, and knowledge on building useful software products that solved real problems.

After multiple failures, my first success came. Raising capital from a real investor. My experience and knowledge had paid off, but now came the hard part: actually delivering the product promised. Having multiple friends in the hospitality industry, I had seen how inefficiently they operated, so I raised money to solve this problem. After multiple rounds of raising capital—around $4 million—I developed a product, built a team and company around the product, and deployed the product into the market. All while continuing to excel as an executive at a major studio.

Although it took a few years, this was a big project, and we built an entire platform across various devices. As CEO of this startup, I wore multiple hats, from product development to sales and quality control. I initially leveraged my corporate job to build this product and company, but toward the end, my learning pace was faster with the startup, so I leveraged it at my corporate job and added more value, which led to more promotions. My hospitality company was in the acquisition conversations and I was out of the day-to-day for some time, which has allowed me to pursue the writing of this book as a side venture. It was eventually acquired during the writing of this book.

Meanwhile, I partnered with a friend to build a simple mobile app, which we funded and sold for $.99 on the App Store. I used everything I learned from the larger hospitality startup company to quickly build and market a mobile app that not only paid for itself but had a very good return on its investment.

Though extremely busy with an executive corporate position and trying to get the hospitality startup off the ground, I was able to find time to get married and become a dad. One of my greatest accomplishments. Since I had built habits and routines on how to juggle a corporate job, building a startup, being married, and being a dad, I felt like I was wasting time I now had that used to be spent on the hospitality startup. So, I went to the drawing board and brainstormed on what my next project was going to be. I came up with a new product idea and planned on building the MVP (minimal viable product) in six months before my son was born, but it ended up taking twenty months. This new product has to do with efficiency, employee engagement, and retention.

I'll get into this latest side venture later in the book, but this is exactly why I'm writing this book. I want to help as many people as I can turn an idea for a software product into reality, and do it quickly by leveraging everything I learned from real success, failures, and experiences. I want to share lessons and advice that are rarely talked about and extremely hard to find online in a cohesive manner. I want you to be in control of your destiny, whatever that might be. I know you are also one idea away from waking up every morning feeling excited.

CHAPTER 3

TIME MANAGEMENT

"Once you have mastered time, you will
understand how true it is that most people
overestimate what they can accomplish in a
year—and underestimate what they can
achieve in a decade!"
Anthony Robbins

What you're about to embark on requires sacrifice, and the only way you will be successful is if you want it bad enough. The most important aspect of making sacrifices is first understanding how you spend your daily and weekly hours. There is a lot written about time management, and every person has their own tricks and best practices. The key is figuring out what works for you.

At the end of the day, no matter how smart, how fortunate, how privileged, or how educated you are, time is the equalizing factor that levels the playing field. It's all about building good habits and using time wisely—which people equate to working hard. Some people confuse working hard with having to stay up all night for months and working sixteen-hour days on a regular basis. This is not sustainable and unhealthy. Working hard means having good habits, so while the people you are competing with are binge-watching the next season of *Stranger Things,* you are drafting your plan, testing a new release, figuring out sales strategy, or doing whatever the next thing is you have to do TODAY. I guarantee that if you are enjoying the process of bringing your idea to life and you are doing it for the right reason, it is not going to feel like hard work.

There are 168 hours in a week. If you spend the average of eight hours sleeping, that leaves you with 112 hours every week. Let's start with your sleeping. You are either an early riser or a late-night crawler. I myself am an early riser. I'm most energetic and fresh in the morning, and it was important for me to identify that about myself. You need to be honest with yourself and figure out when you are most energetic, alert, and productive. This is important, as it shapes most of the habits you will have to form.

Now, how many hours do you actually sleep every night? Is it eight? Seven? Ten? You can use apps like SleepCycle to track your sleep and get to a scientific answer. A lot of what I have read shows that adults need about seven hours of sleep, so you need to form new habits to get your sleep to about seven hours a day. Use alarm clocks and build discipline to form consistent sleeping habits no matter if it's a weekday or the weekend. There is no such thing as weekends for what you are trying to do. If you are already getting less than seven hours of sleep every night ask yourself if you are energetic, focused, and have a clear mind. If you do, you are at an advantage, as you have more hours available to you during the week. If you don't, you need to change your habits to get that extra hour or two of sleep. You have to be alert and focused to be successful in creating a product and launching your own company while excelling at a job that might be funding your venture.

Once you get your sleeping to a habit of seven hours a night with consistent sleep and wake times, you are now giving yourself 119 hours a week to work with. A lot can be done in 119 hours, so let's break this down:

- Forty-nine hours of sleeping
- Forty-five hours at your job (includes commute)

- Fifteen hours with family and friends
- Ten hours rest, relaxation, hobbies
- Ten hours running errands/Dr. appointments/health

After all the above, you still have thirty-nine hours left in a week to immerse yourself in the development of your idea and product. Let me share with you what my weekday schedule was like when I was deep into my hospitality side venture.

My day would start around 6 a.m. The first thing I did was a five-minute meditation session. This did not mean I got a yoga pad and listened to some guru. I would walk outside, close my eyes, take deep breaths of fresh air, and let positive thoughts go through my head. Visualizing success, being on the beach in the Caribbean, and just being thankful for my family and health. I am not into the yoga culture, but because the days were so jam-packed, I found meditation helped me remember what was most important. This was very helpful, as it kept me calm, grounded, and collected all day. My team at my corporate job would always tell me that the leadership quality they learned from me was to stay calm during a crisis—not only did it keep the team calm but it also showed them they could trust my leadership.

After meditation, I would check emails. Both my corporate job and my side venture meant dealing with people overseas, so if there was something urgent, I wanted to know about it right away. I get about 500 work-related emails a day. Some are read-only while others need my response. I would spend thirty minutes early in the morning looking at the new emails and scanning for anything urgent. I would then schedule thirty-minute conference calls around 7 a.m. regarding my side venture. This was primarily with the development team. While on the call, I would eat a quick breakfast, which usually involved eggs. Once the conference call ended, I would review my to-do list for my side venture and see what items I could knock out in thirty minutes. I would then spend thirty minutes with my wife if she was awake, feed the dog, water plants in the backyard, or any other simple and quick house chore. Then I would hit the road around 8:30 a.m. for a thirty-minute commute. While in the car, I would either be on another conference call or listening to an audiobook.

Once I got to the office for my corporate job, my focus was primarily on my work. I was not stealing time from that job to work on my side venture. I couldn't even if I wanted to, as my days were filled with meetings, projects, and presentations. I would leave the office around 6 p.m. and again, I would schedule a thirty-minute conference call or listen to an audiobook.

At home, I would spend time with my wife and have dinner, or we would meet friends for dinner at a local restaurant. I would then free up at around 8:30 p.m. and spend two hours working on my side venture. I tried to work out at least twice a week to help my energy level. I also played one hour of basketball a week. Depending on what I was working on at night, if it was during NBA season, I would have the game on the TV in the background. That is how I kept close to the sport I love. My wife and I watched a few shows together as well. I would be in bed by 11 p.m. and repeat it all again the next day.

My weekends were different, but I still got up around 6 a.m. and went to bed around 11 p.m. Only on rare occasions— weddings, birthday parties, or weekend getaways—was I up past 11 p.m. Once I woke up on weekends, I would spend the early morning hours working on my side venture. This was at least until 9 a.m. Then my wife and I would have a nice breakfast, then I would spend two or three hours working on projects or presentations for my corporate job. Then it was time for family and friends. On Sundays, I gave my brain and body a break by doing a fun activity with my wife or friends, watching a game or an episode or two of a show we both enjoyed. I also used weekends to have day-long meetings with the team.

Since everyone involved in the side venture worked in different locations, getting together once a month in a day-long meeting became very important and effective to get everyone on the same page and make sure everyone knew their marching orders for the next four weeks. The most important work-related task on Sundays was reviewing my calendar at 9:30 p.m. for the week so I knew what meetings I had to be ready for. Of course, the to-do list would change as the week went by, but my Sunday night list was pivotal, as it highlighted the most important tasks to accomplish.

Once I became a father, the first three to four months were difficult and I could not stick to my routine, as I had a new eight-pound boss at home, and my wife and I were his servants. Once he started sleeping through the nights, I was able to go back to my routine—albeit modified. I had to decrease my work time so I could be a dad and I absolutely don't regret it. Being a dad is now a priority over work—if you don't have children, take advantage of the time you have and work as much as you can to get ahead and avoid entertaining yourself with what gives you short-term satisfaction. Your time is limited, so make the best of it.

Now you know how I managed my week. This might not work for you, but this isn't the only way to manage your time. The key is to budget your time weekly and make sure you are allocating adequate time for your side venture. It's OK to say no to loved ones and accept the fact that you will have to miss out on certain events. This is one of the sacrifices you have to make if you don't want to be lying on your deathbed with regrets for not ever pursuing your goals and ideas, which could have turned into true passions. If through the process you realize that your side venture is less important than time with friends and family and sacrificing time with them is what you will regret when you are ninety, that is fine. This journey can also be a self-discovery journey where you find out what you are really made of and what truly makes you happy. Happiness is the ultimate goal.

How do you establish routines and time management habits? Let's get into some of the guiding principles that helped me with mine.

Time is not the problem. No matter what you do, you will always have 24 hours in a day, so time management is actually behavior management. It's up to you how you manage the 24 hours. Make this mental shift and focus on creating habits as opposed to checking time.

Figure out what activities and tasks you waste time on and eliminate or minimize them. Do you spend an hour on social media each day? Do you watch multiple hours of TV each day? Do you surf the internet without a purpose? Are you talking to friends on messaging apps all day? Limit these activities and you will quickly have more time to focus on something that is productive or helping you learn and grow. The goal is to change your habits, and by changing your habits, you will use your time more effectively. One way I was able to do this was by setting a weekly goal and holding myself accountable for it. For example, if my goal was to limit TV watching to only six hours for the week, I would keep track of how many actual hours of TV I ended up watching and compare the result to my goal. We will get into business metrics later, but personal metrics also help you change behavior and decisions. After all, what you can't measure you can't manage.

You probably don't have the luxury of having a personal assistant, but you can still find smart ways to delegate and outsource tactical tasks. This helps you manage your time by freeing up your time. Use tools like Fiverr, Freelancer, Task Rabbit, and others to develop relationships with a few people overseas with specific skills. You can then delegate and outsource tasks for a very low cost. For example, you can find someone that is a Powerpoint expert so you don't spend hours trying to make a presentation look polished and professional. Or, you might need some online research conducted so you can understand the size of your addressable market. Use technology to free up your time so you can focus on the most important and strategic aspects of your side venture. You can apply the same approach to your job, but be sure to check your company security policies so you don't share sensitive information when trying to delegate a task to a third party.

You need to have a to-do list. You can use a simple notepad or choose from dozens of fancy apps with loads of features, or use a simpler version of a digital notepad—I personally use Evernote to create and organize my to-do lists. If your week starts on a Monday, by Sunday night you should have a list of key things you need to take care of during the upcoming week. However, once the week starts and more things come up, you have to be disciplined enough to quickly add the new items to the list—especially if an idea pops into your head and you wish to record it right away before you forget it. I personally use Siri to help me capture a note, which will then remind me to update my to-do list or any document once I'm able to.

The goal is that any item added to the list for this week between Sunday night and Friday night is done by the following Sunday. If you can't complete an item on the list during that week, then you are either overcommitting yourself or you are procrastinating. You might not be taking things seriously or the item is not something that belongs on the to-do list. Or, the item might be more of a project instead of a task. For example, "create a business plan" cannot be on your to-do list. This is a strategic project. Instead, break down this project into all the tasks you need to complete in order to complete the project. As an example, "research competitors" will be a task on the to-do list. On Sunday, while reviewing the list, hold yourself accountable for the tasks you did not manage to accomplish during the week.

Now that you have a to-do list, always make sure you are completing the harder, more time-consuming tasks first. This will help you feel productive and you'll have the momentum to tackle the smaller, more simple tasks. Also, in most cases, the harder tasks add more value to your idea and side venture, so it helps to push forward the larger projects.

Don't focus too much on small details—but don't be sloppy either. You still need to approach everything with integrity, excellence, and professionalism, but getting caught up in the small details and trying to perfect everything will only slow you down. Also, what you perceive as perfect today won't be perfect a week from now, so in most cases, you are chasing after something that just can't be reached.

In today's society, we are surrounded by technology, which makes it that much harder for us to shut it down and be out of reach. Voice call, FaceTime, email, text, app notifications, etc. distract us. Setting aside two to four hours a day as your "distraction-free" time can be helpful. Set expectations with family, friends, and colleagues that you will not respond to non-emergency requests during this period. You'll be surprised how quickly everyone will adapt and how free you will feel to have a few hours of uninterrupted time to yourself to work on the hardest items on your list.

You also need to create smart personal systems. I don't mean you have to build your own software. Personal systems are approaches and methodologies to situations that are unique to you—how you read, respond to, delete, and archive emails is your own personal system; how you organize your desktop is your own personal system; how you organize your closet is your own personal system. Establish personal systems that are effective and do not take a lot of time. For example, some people take a lot of time each day moving all their emails from their inbox to some folder structure. In most cases, you will never need to look for these emails, and if you do, search tools in all email clients are so robust that you can find anything you want fairly quickly.

Don't try to do too much at once—be smart in your multitasking. For example, working on a presentation and working with the artists helping you with the presentation at the same time is smart multitasking. If you are testing a new release of a feature while taking notes as you are designing a complementary feature makes sense. It does not make sense to work on a PowerPoint presentation while researching the new refrigerator you want to buy. In short, you can chunk together similar and related tasks to get more done. I usually do this with no more than three tasks, as any more than three related tasks can become too much and you are no longer able to focus and be effective. If you cannot complete a task with 100 percent satisfactory results, you are doing too much.

And lastly, if you are in your twenties or early thirties, single, and partying on a regular basis, you need to make a complete change of lifestyle—and in some cases, friends—right away. You need to chase what matters, and what matters is not at parties, raves, music festivals, and nightclubs. These are all distractions that will slow you down.

I view life in thirds. The first third of your life is about growing into an adult, education, establishing your foundation, understanding what you want in life, and aggressively going after it by working hard. The second third of your life is about using the momentum you have established to become financially successful so you have the freedom of doing what you want both on a personal level and a professional level. If you have dreamed of making an independent movie, this is your time to get creative and do things you have always dreamed about. This is only possible if you work hard during the first third of your life to establish your foundation and habits. This is why partying on a weekly basis during the first third of your life is a dream killer that is almost impossible to recover from. It is also a huge waste of time, as you are probably in bed all Saturday or Sunday recovering from the night before. The last third of your life is about giving back and making a positive impact on other people's lives.

You will have moments where you feel overwhelmed. Don't let this get the best of you. Make sure you get away every three to four months to decompress, energize your mind, and read as much as possible. Books will unlock secrets to help you along your adventure.

If you are reading this book, I believe you are already trying to be more deliberate and calculated in your approach to building better habits so you can use your time more effectively. You will fail, especially at the beginning, but as long as you have established strong habits, moving on to the next idea will be easy. Remember, you are one idea away from freedom.

Visit the link below for a chapter summary and resources related to this chapter.

www.ch3resources.sideadventure.com

CHAPTER 4

THE FOUNDATION

"Do what you have to do until you can do
what you want to do."
Oprah Winfrey

"Always deliver more than expected."
Larry Page, co-founder of Google

If you have recently started a new job, you have a clean slate and can follow the strategies I'm about to share. If you have been at your job for more than a year, you might be carrying some unwanted baggage, but you can still follow and apply these strategies to turn things around or build on your existing momentum. The goal of this chapter is to show you how you can establish a foundation, set good examples, align with the right people, and earn autonomy. Everyone wants autonomy, but it has to be earned. When you are trying to pursue your own venture, the flexibility you gain because of autonomy is critical.

I was twenty-three when I landed my first real corporate job. From my internship, I learned that I needed to make a good first impression. I tried to do this with my immediate manager and my manager's boss. I would overdeliver and be as reliable and resourceful as I could. I was friendly and collaborative with everyone else, but it didn't cross my mind at the time that when building a personal brand, I needed to treat and approach every person and situation with the same personal brand values.

Within the first year, a colleague of mine got promoted and was now my manager. I thought, *Do I have to start all over again to establish my personal brand?* That's when I realized that I couldn't pick and choose who I over-delivered for and who I didn't. It's important to have a single personal brand, so not only do you not have to prove yourself every time you get a new manager, but also, that is how opportunities will come to you, as other managers will want to recruit you.

Once I changed my mindset, the promotion opportunities started coming my way. As I got more visibility into mid- and senior-level management, I started paying close attention to the various leadership styles. I noticed the caring leader, the mentor leader, the technical leader, the strategic leader, the visionary leader, the introvert leader, and the extrovert leader. Leaders that led by example, leaders that led by seniority, leaders that lifted people up, leaders that led by fear, and leaders that pushed people down. I also began paying close attention to who potential future leaders were. I was already a big fan of self-help books, but this fascinated me, so I dove deep into leadership books.

I wanted to establish a relationship with and learn more about the people around me, so I began requesting lunch and coffee meetings. With each encounter, I made sure I was listening more and talking less, trying to find things we had in common. Sometimes it worked better than other times, but they all knew my name, and when they heard my name in a positive light, it just added to my personal brand image.

There was one specific senior executive that stood out amongst the crowd. He was charismatic, personable, intelligent, practical, strategic, and knew how to approach difficult conversations and how to cast a vision. There were other leaders I liked, but I felt that our personalities and the way we operated did not match. I also observed how this leader was respected by everyone else, so I knew that I had to align with him. I made a deliberate decision to make sure I raised my hand and said *yes* when called upon by this leader. As a result, he became my unofficial boss and mentor. He guided me through challenges and decisions, and finally, with promotions, he became my official boss.

When it comes to any job, you want to have a boss that makes you feel empowered, values your perspective even if it differs from theirs, and challenges you by putting you in situations that will push you to grow. Avoid working for somebody who leads by fear and doesn't value your opinion, even if it means passing up on a promotion.

As I was navigating this complex environment of leaders, future leaders, and colleagues, it was difficult to always make sure my personal brand was represented correctly. At first it bothered me, but soon I learned to just listen and absorb it as feedback. Some became learning opportunities while others were far from reality, but instead of getting upset, I took it upon myself to change that individual's perception. I believe it was the athlete in me drawing from the mental toughness of Kobe Bryant and Michael Jordan, two athletes I admire because of how they approached the game, which made them stand out from other NBA athletes. It also helped that, through all of this, I had my friend Michael going through similar situations, as we worked for the same organization. We have very similar mindsets and philosophies. We were each other's bouncing board, and we still are to this day.

Let's break things down into more practical advice and strategies that you can start applying to your own professional life:

Establishing a foundation. Just like on a first date, it's pivotal to make a good first impression. But instead of courting one person, in a business environment, you are courting multiple people all together—which is not an easy task. The mistake I have seen many people make is that they usually focus on impressing their immediate boss and downplay or ignore everyone else. Speed of change has never been this rapid. Your boss today might not be your boss in six months. They might not even be in the same organization anymore, so simply impressing your immediate boss is a big mistake. You need a more inclusive strategy. Initially, you need to have a mindset that everyone you work with might one day be that director, VP, CEO, or president you report to. Do not underestimate anyone, as there are many layers involved to successfully move up the ladder.

Your number one priority should be to establish a relationship with the people you work with. Make a list of people you wish to impress and, once you have that list, reach out to each person to set up a thirty-minute coffee meeting. Some of you might be in a small organization and you only have five people to meet with, but some of you might be in a large corporation and you have fifty people to meet with. Set an aggressive deadline to complete these meetings, as rescheduling will happen and you don't want this initial step to take months.

When you reach out to these individuals, your approach should be treating these people like a client. Your actual email will sound different based on the person's seniority and title. Let me share with you a few examples.

For colleagues and others not in management, your request might sound something like this. "Hi John, if you have thirty minutes, I would like to buy you a coffee sometime this week. It would be great if I could pick your brain about how you established yourself and any other advice you might have for me."

The primary goal of this meeting is to establish a relationship. To do this, you should be listening 70 percent of the time and talking 30 percent of the time. Be genuine and try to get to know the person. Find a common interest you can have an engaging conversation about. Maybe both of you recently had a baby. Maybe both of you are into sports and like the same team or are rivals. Maybe you recently watched the same movie. There will always be a common interest; it is your job to ask questions and listen to find it.

Once you establish rapport, you can then move on to asking for advice. You want advice on who they think the best executives are, how long he or she has been with the company, and any general advice they have for you. What you should take away from the given advice is which executives are liked. These will be candidates to be mentors. Ask your colleague, What are some problems in the organization? What are some things you have issues with that I can help you with?

The next group of people you want to meet with are managers and midlevel executives. This group will be smaller than your initial group. Your email to this group may sound something like this. "Hi Mary, I'm fairly new to the organization and as I have been meeting different people, your name has come up as someone who is highly respected and gives good advice, so I was wondering if I could buy you a coffee and absorb your knowledge."

Just as in the first group, your primary goal is to establish a relationship. Listen and ask questions to find common interests. Then ask the person how they got the role they are in now, the challenges in their team, and what they think gets people promoted. The goal is to understand the problems this person is facing and the road they took to be in a leadership position. End with asking about senior leadership and who they like and why. Again, your goal here is to identify potential mentors.

The last group of people you want to meet with are senior leaders. These are typically people in VP and above roles. You will probably only have a few names in this group based on what you heard in your prior meetings. Your email reaching out to this group might sound something like this. "Hi Jenny, my name is _____ and I work on _____'s team. I have heard many good things about what a great leader and mentor you are and was wondering if I could buy you a coffee and pick your brain."

Your goal with these meetings is to see if this leader is someone you would like to have as a mentor. Ask about the problems they have in their organization and who they think the up-and-coming leaders are. Establish a rapport as you did in previous meetings, then ask questions that get you to your desired outcome. You will close the loop on this process by making sure you have met or are going to meet with anyone this senior leader believes is an up-and-coming leader. Don't get intimidated by the person's position. People love to be flattered—especially successful people—so by reaching out to this group, you are actually feeding what they are looking for at this stage in their life and career. Making a difference in people's lives and leaving a legacy is what most people in this group are thinking about, so don't let false assumptions about people not willing to help hold you back.

Be sure to take notes and study what problems people you interviewed face—aim to solve one problem per year. This is exactly what I did when I got hired at my first corporate job. I'll never forget the words of a specific SVP when I had my meeting with him. He told me that the larger the organization, the more problems there are, so it's very easy to get noticed by upper management. Just solve these problems and promotions will come your way. He was right! I was only months into the job, but I had a long list of problems I had documented. The problem I focused on was on the bottom half of the list. Other problems that I had ranked higher I did not feel like I understood well enough yet nor was I in a position to solve them. You will most likely be in a similar situation, but these problems do not go away quickly, so don't feel rushed to tackle them all. It's better to focus on one and hit it out of the park than spread yourself thin and do a half-ass job.

While you are trying to continue to learn the job you were hired for and solve the one problem you are focusing on, you must not forget that you are still in the phase of establishing or re-establishing a good impression. You are your brand, and a positive brand will go a long way. When you think of Apple, you think of individual creativity. When you think of BMW, you think of the ultimate driving machine. You want people to associate positive attributes with your name as well. Attributes that I believe are equal to success are: reliable, self-starter, honest, can-do attitude, driven.

Reliability starts with being present. Someone that doesn't show up and calls in sick regularly is hard to be viewed as reliable. I did not look at the sick days the company gave me as additional vacation days and, to this day, I only use my sick days when I am truly sick or have to take care of a sick family member.

Being reliable also means following through and getting things done. No matter what the project or request is, you have to deliver on time or early and exceed the quality expectation of whomever you are delivering to. Be resourceful. Remember that your brand is a collective perception, and word-of-mouth advertising counts. There is a feeling of accomplishment and pride when I impress people and, regardless of whether I was completing a task for my colleague or boss, I went above and beyond to impress the person, which eventually helped my brand. Figure out what drives you to get things done and exceed expectations.

Be honest, and don't get caught up in work-related gossip. There is nothing wrong with having friends at work and spending lunches and breaks with them, but avoid gossiping.

I made it a point to not be involved in conversations that negatively portrayed someone else. Remember that if you have a conversation with someone about someone else, that person might assume that you were talking about them when they were not present. Be ethical and hold yourself to higher standards than being caught up in a conversation that centers around negativity in the workplace. More opportunities will be presented to you if you are ethical.

I'm pretty sure you have heard the saying that if you are being offered a great opportunity just say yes, then figure out how to execute and deliver. This is very true. The layer that I would like to add to this is that you should say yes strategically after a certain point in your career. You can only do this if you are clear about your short-term and long-term goals and what you want your life to mean. For example, if your goal is to become a world-famous chef and you have outlined how you will get there and along the way you are presented with an opportunity that is in commercial real estate, you have to think strategically to see if this fits in your plan or not. If this opportunity will derail you, then you have to say no. If you planned to find capital to open your own restaurant then maybe you say yes, as this might be the opportunity that gives you the liquid cash you need to open up that restaurant.

In 2006, I agreed to work on a project of which I only knew the code name, which was given to the project by Steve Jobs. It was related to the launch of the first iTunes movie store. I was so glad I had said yes. All of a sudden, I was on the cutting edge of digital film distribution. A startup within a large corporation. It was right up my alley and helped me develop and learn many key skills that allowed me to take this single project into a full-blown department in a few years.

Add value. Although we will focus more on this topic later on, adding value to a project will quickly get you to shine among the rest and hopefully lead to a promotion within your workplace.

How to get promoted. Now that you know how to set a positive first impression or re-establish yourself and build your own personal brand, let's get into some specific strategies to help you get promoted. Promotion can lead to more autonomy, but you have to learn how to manage people and be a leader. Leadership is a critical skill you need to develop if you are going to have a chance at successfully pursuing your own side venture.

Know the rules of the game. What gets you promoted at one company is not necessarily what gets you promoted at another company. A company that has been in business for decades might have slower promotion cycles compared to a younger one. A company in growth mode will have more promotional opportunities than a company in cost-saving mode. Some companies have clear guidelines for promotions while others don't. Every company has different qualities and achievements they consider as promotion material.

Your job is to have a clear understanding of where your company and organization fall. Meet with your HR representative and make it known to them that you are interested in moving up and you want to understand how promotion requests are evaluated, what achievements and successes qualify for a promotion, and if promotions are approved easily or not. Communicate with your colleagues and get their feedback on how they think promotions work and their overall feelings about the health of promotional activity. Then, meet with at least two executives to get their feedback on what they look for before promoting a team member. Find out the skills and qualities they value, why they would push for a promotion for someone in their team, and whether promotions are an easy process for them. Make sure you take notes during these conversations.

Be brutally honest. Now that you have a good sense of what it takes to be promoted, you have to be brutally honest with yourself and assess your weaknesses and strengths. If you are not sure where you stand in certain skills, ask for feedback and be open to receiving constructive criticism. Write down the skills you need to acquire and plan how you are going to acquire them. Outside of resources your company might offer, there are so many resources on the web that can help you acquire new skills.

Be your own PR rep. One of the worst mistakes you can make is assuming that people in the position to make decisions about your career will notice your hard work and reward you for it. This is far from the truth, especially in large organizations. You have worked hard to establish your own brand, now it is time to be your own PR representative and get people to notice your brand. Commercial brands need marketing, sales, and PR to generate revenue and so do you. You can use two simple strategies to do this without coming across as that person who is always boasting about themselves.

Establish a cadence where you send an email to your immediate manager of your accomplishments during that period. Align your list of personal accomplishments with what you have already heard to be accomplishments the company leadership looks at highly. Become comfortable enough with your manager so that you establish an open line of communication, which will allow you to express exactly what your goals are—don't assume they will just figure it out. Do presentations for leadership that demonstrate your accomplishments. If the presentation is successful, ask your manager to allow you to present it to a larger group in the future.

Create allies. Leverage the steps you took when you were setting a good impression, creating your brand, and establishing relationships to get the right people on your side. By now you should have identified who the influencers in your organization are. These are the people whose opinions matter more. Some of these people will be in the room when promotions are being discussed. By having the right influencers as your ally, you have basically done the equivalent of creating such a great product that word-of-mouth marketing is helping it grow.

Continue to add value. Keep the list of your problems current and be strategic on which ones you tackle. The problems you solve will have a positive impact on your company and organization, but they will also make life easier for certain individuals. Therefore, you should aim to make life easier for the influencers, your boss, and other leaders. This will help you create allies as well. You should make it a point to present, to whomever is interested, the problem you solved and how. This will help you play the role of your own PR rep as well.

Help your boss. No matter how it might be perceived, everyone has a personal agenda, which is OK. As long as the agenda is not malicious, everyone should have something they are personally pursuing. Sometimes people might have the same intention but are taking different approaches. This can cause a conflict, but don't take things personally. Your boss will have some kind of agenda as well. Try to understand what it is and help him achieve it. Not only does this help you create an alliance with your boss, but if your boss gets promoted, you might as well.

The big picture. In your pursuit of a promotion, don't lose sight of the big picture. You want a promotion to make money so you can pursue your own side ventures but also gain autonomy. If you know a leader is a micro-manager, you should stay clear from that team. If you have followed the strategies that I have outlined, you should already have some autonomy because of the respect you have garnered for yourself. Do not get frustrated if a promotion is not happening. There can be many reasons, but if you are not viewed as promotion material, you have to make a big decision: stick around or move on. Whatever you decide, keep in mind that time is the most valuable commodity, and you have to be in a place that allows you to apply my suggested strategies, whether at your current job or not.

After going through the above, which can take months if not a couple of years, you should be in very good standing with your company or organization. It's now time to use your good standing and improve on some key skills that you will need to increase your probability of success in your side venture.

Networking. You have already been doing this, but now it's time to take it up a notch. Increase the number of senior-level people you meet within your own company or vendors your company has relationships with. You need to have executive presence, so you need to have direct contact with established executives to learn from. How you present yourself, your vocabulary, how you articulate your thoughts and ideas, and your body language are key when meeting investors, clients, and partners for your own side venture, so be mindful of that. Everyone has different styles and there isn't a black-and-white approach, but the more you interact with people who are in a senior position, the more you will get a good sense of what works and what doesn't.

Presentations. I can't stress this enough. You need to become an excellent presenter. If you have a fear of public speaking, start by doing small presentations to overcome your fear. Do a presentation on your family, your childhood, your favorite athlete. The objective is to get comfortable taking command of the room because presentations will be a key tool in your sales effort for your side venture. You can even partner with one or more people to ease you into it.

Whether you are selling to an investor or a client, as a startup CEO you will be doing a lot of selling. We will get into sales in a later chapter, but being comfortable with giving presentations is the start of getting you ready. I remember doing presentations on topics I knew a lot about but were not work-related. That led to doing presentations on successful projects and eventually big-pitch presentations. By the time I had to do a presentation for an investor, I felt so confident in my speaking and presentation abilities that my confidence alone helped me hit it out of the park.

Managing vendors. Understanding how to manage a vendor is extremely important, especially if you are not a software engineer, which means you will need to hire a vendor to help you build your product. In my role in the corporate world, managing vendors was a primary responsibility, and I later realized how beneficial this was when I was dealing with an offshore software development firm. If you do not deal with vendors in your current role, talk to people who manage vendors. Ask them about the tools they use, how they evaluate vendors, how they deal with performance issues, and what the challenges are. The goal is to familiarize yourself with how different teams within your organization or company manage vendors. We will dive deep into managing an offshore software development vendor in a later chapter, as this alone can cause your side venture to fail if you don't understand some key fundamentals.

RFP. The acronym stands for Request for Proposal and it's the first step in engaging with a vendor. This is where you provide details of your project and request answers to some key questions to help you evaluate and select the vendor you will work with. I will go into details of how to approach an RFP with a software development vendor but, at this stage, I want you to become familiar with how your company or organization handles RFPs. Of course, cost is a big factor in all RFPs, but what are some other areas your company considers? Depending on the size of your company, the RFP might be conducted by a sourcing team, a finance team, or the manager of a department, so find out who you can get in contact with to help you get familiarized with the process.

Metrics. A successfully managed business will have metrics to keep a pulse on every key performance indicator—or KPIs. Find out what kind of metrics are being kept, why they are being kept, how they are being used, and how the integrity of the data is maintained. This should give you a good overview of real-life business examples. You can couple this with what you will learn about metrics in a later chapter to set up and manage the right metrics for your side venture. After all, you can't manage what you can't measure. Tip: if your company or organization is not using metrics and making data-driven decisions, once you have a better understanding of metrics and KPI, you should propose a business change, which will help you stand out from the rest.

Hiring and firing. To no surprise, hiring is always easier than firing for most people. We will get into the specifics around this topic, specifically for startups, but you should use this opportunity to get on interview panels and get some real-life experience interviewing people. Pay attention to questions that are asked, how different people answer them, and pay even closer attention to your biases and how you might be making instant judgments without knowing. When it comes to your side venture, you want people that bring different perspectives and experience to the table.

Sales and marketing. If your role is not in sales or marketing, your job is to become familiar with how the sales and marketing teams function in your company. The details might be irrelevant to a software startup, but there are some fundamentals in sales and marketing that are universal. Again, we will cover this topic in more depth in a later chapter, but having some familiarity with how a real business handles sales and marketing will be truly beneficial, not only for how to come up with sales and marketing ideas, but also for learning about execution, scaling, and sustaining a campaign or process, which is more important than the idea. Whether you like it or not, as a startup founder you will have to be a shrewd salesperson to sell your idea to investors, build a team, and sell the product.

Software development. This is by far the most important learning opportunity. Most of you don't have a software background and do not work in IT or technology. To gain an understanding of how software is built, you should volunteer to help with a project where a business system is being built. You want to understand the vocabulary being used, what tools are being leveraged to manage the project, and the roles and responsibilities of the various people involved. Understand the methodologies and the why behind them. Align yourself with someone that can give you more insight into the process beyond the role you are playing so you can see what is happening behind the curtains.

In addition, talk to the eventual users of this new business system to get feedback from them on their challenges and issues. Once this project is done, get involved in another software project if possible. These projects will have the most impact in preparing you for kicking off your side venture and building a prototype and MVP (minimum viable product). An MVP is the version of your product with enough features for your early customers to allow for real scenario usage and feedback gathering.

If your side venture does not work out or you decide entrepreneurship is not for you, these strategies will still help you advance your career in the corporate world. You will gain MBA-level knowledge but with real experience and without the debt. And hopefully, you'll become the leader everyone wants to align with and be mentored by.

Visit the link below for a chapter summary and resources related to this chapter.

www.ch4resources.sideadventure.com

Chapter 5

Managing Personal Relationships

"Great spirits have always encountered violent
opposition from mediocre minds."
Albert Einstein

"Being realistic is the most common path to
mediocrity."
Will Smith

When I began my professional journey almost twenty years ago, I was single with very few responsibilities. In these twenty years, I went through relationships and personal growth, reduced my circle of friends, got engaged, got married, and became a dad. I now have some hard responsibilities for the rest of my life. You have probably gone through all or some of these stages as well. In this chapter, I want to talk about how to get into and maintain healthy relationships while trying to give it your all at your job and side venture, how to surround yourself with supportive friends and family, and what to do with unsupportive people in your circle that can deter you from your goals and dreams.

Let's face it, if you want to excel in your job and pursue your own side venture, you must be part of a special breed of individuals. Our conversations consist of discussing ideas, other entrepreneurs, seminars, and daydreaming about when everything comes together and what we will do when we have financial freedom. And the rest of our time we spend obsessing about the book we are reading or listening to, the online training class we are taking, the how-to videos we are watching, and the to-do list that we can't wait to get started on.

We work long hours and, being physically and mentally drained, often say no to events, hanging out with friends, and seeing family members. How we go about our day becomes a habit—some good and some bad. Until I met my wife, I kept telling myself I was too busy to look for love. Now I see it was simply an excuse and I just needed to prioritize my love life. If you are making this excuse as well, you might be masking your loneliness by keeping yourself busy. Why would anybody want to date an entrepreneur? All we talk about is work, our latest idea, the latest thing we have learned from a book or seminar. In some cases, we are crazy enough to quit a very stable job to launch a startup that statistically has a low chance of success. But I have also learned that we have some particularly good attributes that people might not see in us right away. We are driven, focused, resilient, and passionate. So, what are some things I had to learn and do to maintain a healthy romantic relationship, surround myself with the right friends, and know which family members I could rely on for support?

Let's begin with how to start and maintain a healthy romantic relationship. When I first started dating my wife, I listened carefully to understand what was important to her. I soon realized that she was a foodie and loved trying new restaurants. She enjoyed traveling, being out and about, and did not like staying home for lengthy periods of time. She was family-oriented and wanted to make sure she was in regular contact with her family members. Having a positive relationship with friends was also extremely important to her. She was not about material things but occasionally enjoyed buying herself something nice.

Making her my priority was easy for me. We enjoyed our weekly date nights—even now that we are parents—and we often invite friends as well, which makes her happy because she enjoys keeping in touch with them. We value our time together, even if it's just getting breakfast at a local Starbucks—which is where I did most of the writing for this book.

Given her love of travel, we choose not to spend money on material things and instead save up for wonderful vacations and getaways. For example, before we got married, we went on a trip to the South of France. We've visited Italy—on our honeymoon—Spain, Hawaii, Mexico, and the Caribbean to name a few, not to mention the many states we've traveled to in the United States. Since we believe in having an honest and open line of communication, she knows it's important to me not to fall behind on work-related matters, which is why she respects my decision to bring my laptop on vacation and allows me the freedom of working for a couple of hours here and there. She places high value on family, so we visit parents regularly. I'm so thankful for my wife for helping me realize the importance of this value. Based on my experience, let me break down what it takes to have a happy, stable, and durable romantic relationship.

Make your significant other a top priority. This does not mean forget everything else, spending every single waking minute with this person, or putting yourself on the back burner. Having a person be your top priority starts with communication, and the most important part of communication is the ability to listen to what is important to them. Making your significant other a top priority means respecting their needs and priorities. Also, focus on quality time and plan your activities accordingly.

Encourage their independence. Your significant other had a life before you, and they should not have to give it up just because you are part of it now. Tell each other what your expectations are and what is acceptable to you, and establish a trustworthy and mutually respectful relationship so that you can still have time to focus on what matters to you and pursue your entrepreneurial dreams.

Whenever possible, I involve my wife in what I'm doing by bouncing ideas off of her, showing her mockups and prototypes, getting her involved in user testing, and most importantly, including her in fun activities such as parties, dinners, and business trips. By involving her, she sees that I value her opinion and that she is part of whatever I'm planning. She is also in the loop of what is going on with the project and feels like an insider. If she already knows a big week is coming up, she helps me with it, even if the help is giving me as much time as I need to perform work-related tasks.

Be careful not to bombard them with complaints about things going wrong, challenges with people, and general issues. This can manifest itself in the relationship. Find the right balance. I have seen situations where the husband or wife started working in the startup as an employee. With the right setup, this can be rewarding, but I have seen it not work out as well. When a couple works together, you have to be even more conscious about giving them their independence and alone time, as spending all day and night with the same person is not an easy thing to do for most people.

Achieving a work-life balance has proven to be challenging in today's society because we're always connected. Back in the 1960s and 1970s, most of us would wake up and spend some time at home, then go to work, then come back home for the evening and the night. If you were in the office or place of work from 9 a.m. to 9 p.m., you were working too much and had to balance your hours better. The phrase I prefer to use today is work-life integration. Mix work and pleasure. With the technology we have at our disposal, it is easy to go on vacation and spend two or three hours of peak productivity on work. This was not possible a few decades ago. Don't break up your day into life and work. Work is part of your life and you should integrate the two in a way that makes it feel like one thing. For me, I might spend ten hours working in a day, but it is never ten consecutive hours. I mix work and pleasure, which keeps me energized and rarely mentally drained.

Some of you might already have families, so not only do you have to be a husband or wife, but also a mom or dad. You might be thinking that you have lost your opportunity to pursue your entrepreneurial dreams. This is far from the truth. Most people assume that startups can only be successful because the founders are young and single and can devote all their time to the business. Yes, it does take a lot of hard work and sacrifices to pursue your own side venture and even more hard work to turn it into a successful business that you are passionate about and makes you happy and fulfilled, but having a family gives you a massive "why" that can sustain your drive and motivation. After all, what better reason to win in life than for your family? Also, the support you can get from your family makes the hard times easier to deal with.

MIT research shows that the average age of a startup founder is forty-two years old and that older founders are more successful than young ones. Not only do the older founders have a bigger why, but they have more real-world experience.

Now that you know it is possible to pursue your own side venture even if you have a family, you have to make sure you prepare your family for this journey by mastering the art of working smarter, not harder. This starts with your corporate job. Two ways to do this is by automating what can be automated and delegating. If you are in a managerial position, you need to focus on hiring people that are smarter than you to make it easier to delegate. The goal here is to be efficient at your job so you are not staying late or taking work home.

Next, you need to establish routines and habits to eliminate the need to constantly plan your days and weeks. When it comes to tasks related to your side venture or even certain tasks around the house, find a way to outsource them. If you are financially stable, you can hire a full-time assistant, or a virtual assistant, which will cost less. At the very least, you need to outsource tasks to freelancers using tools like Taskrabbit, Fiverr, Freelancer, Upwork, and Thumbtack. These are a few of the tools I use, but there are many others that easily enable you to outsource tasks. If you are not in a position to do this because of financial reasons, then you are not in a place to start a side venture. You first need to work on your finances, which I will go into in-depth in an upcoming chapter.

The last big way to work smarter is to communicate, communicate, communicate. The most obvious reason this helps you work smarter—both at work and for your side venture—is because if directions are not clear, you will waste time having to re-do tasks and projects. Take time to be clear and direct in your communication up front. It will save you a lot of hours on the backend.

If a decision you are about to make may have an impact on your family, then you must include them in that decision. Not only use them as a bouncing board to flesh out your idea, but make sure you hear out their concerns, requests, and hopefully cheers. There is no better support than your family, so show them that they are your priority. This will dramatically increase the level of support you will get, even if they don't fully agree with your crazy idea of maybe one day in the future leaving your job.

Next is making sure you communicate and are transparent about how you will be spending your time and getting on the same page with your significant other on what you are responsible for when it comes to the house and kids. Your kids and significant other will need your attention but remember, it is quality over quantity. Set specific hours during the week where, unless you are traveling, they will have 100 percent of your attention. Let your family know what a potential workday looks like. As we discussed before, integrating your work into your life is how you will be more efficient while also spending quality time with your family.

One of the ways to do this is by putting family activities into your work calendar. Not only does it act as a good reminder, but you can have a single view of your daily schedule. A very important family activity that you should plan is your annual vacation. This is a must, as it is quality time with the family, but if you have done everything else according to plan, you will still be able to get some work in. This is part of how you will be spending your time and it shows that you are making time for the family.

Getting up before everyone else will give you an hour or two of quiet time to work on your side venture. You can also stay up an hour or two after everyone has fallen asleep. You won't have to worry about giving anyone attention or doing things around the house. If you communicate in advance that this is what you will be doing, even on those occasional days where your significant other wakes up earlier than usual or falls asleep later than usual, expectation has been set, so it is less likely you will be interrupted. Please remember that waking up early or sleeping late cannot come at the sacrifice of less sleep. You need six or seven hours of sleep each night to stay sharp, focused, and productive. Anything less than this on a regular basis is likely to backfire on you.

And last but not least, you should spend five to ten minutes doing a meditation exercise. Focus on relaxation and gratitude. The relaxation part will help you get ready for a busy day so you do not feel overwhelmed and stressed, while the gratitude part will keep you grounded and remind you of how lucky you are to be alive.

We have touched on strategies to help you maintain a healthy romantic and family relationship, but let's talk about how to deal with those unsupportive members of your extended family and friends. When it comes to your circle of friends and family, they typically fall into three categories. Those few you look up to because they have achieved something that you want to achieve—they inspire you and directly or indirectly challenge you because they are proof that it is possible. Your goal should be to network and increase this circle.

Then, there are those you spend the most time with because you are at the same level and relate to each other one way or another. If you are far from where you thought you would be at this stage in your life, this circle of friends might falsely justify where you are in your life. If this circle is dramatically bigger than the circle you look up to, then you are probably missing out on some positive peer pressure.

The last circle of people are the ones that look up to you. The ideal scenario would be that you have more people you look up to than those you might consider to be below your level and look up to you until you have achieved massive success. Once most of your traditional circle of family and friends place you in their top circle as someone they look up to, there will be many other naysayers and haters. People will await your failure, as that helps them justify their lack of accomplishments or why they have not been able to pursue their goals and dreams.

They will feed you negative thought patterns like, "I tried this and it's much harder than you think." Or, "Don't most businesses fail within the first five years?" "You're working too much. What if it ends up being for nothing?" "You seem to care more about your business than your friends and family." These are the people that are waiting to say "I told you so." But the irony is that as soon as you have some level of success, the same people will say, "I knew you would make it."

Your goal is not to prove them wrong—even though it'd feel good. You need to stay focused on why you want to pursue a side venture and work harder than others. Leverage these people to fine-tune and master your communication and sales skills. If you are not able to clearly articulate your ideas to friends and family, you will have a very hard time convincing investors to invest in you and customers to buy from you. You can also use friends and family to find flaws in your overall idea and plan so you can improve on it.

Ask yourself if the person giving you the advice or making a comment has achieved something you want. Evaluate the validity of what you are hearing, as not all advice is equal and you don't have the time to look into everything. For example, what you hear from your eighty-year-old grandma—as important as it might be—who was a homemaker all her life might weigh less than your uncle who has a successful small business. Accept constructive criticism and develop a thick skin because you will hear plenty of "No."

Part of not taking things personally is not getting defensive. You don't want to get into an argument with family and friends. That's a no-win situation. They might have a hard time seeing your point of view, especially if it is different from what they are familiar with. For example, if your side venture is to build an audience on YouTube, family and friends with a traditional view of a career will not be able to wrap their head around what you are trying to do. Getting into an argument with them to convince them you are right will not work. Do the hard work and make it happen. This is how you will eventually win them over.

Identify your core four or five friends that you have an authentic friendship with. It is true that you become who you spend the most time with, so choose wisely. These authentic relationships will be there to support you, even if they don't fully agree with you at first. Most importantly, they will take joy in celebrating your wins with you. It is the opinion and feedback of these core friends that you should value.

Be honest with your friends and tell them how you wish to be supported. Those who do end up supporting you based on your ask are who you want to keep close. Those that don't you want to distance yourself from, when possible. This also helps you establish boundaries with your extended family and friends. If they see that you are serious, they will treat you differently than if you joke about your side venture.

Similar to your immediate family, you should leverage your extended family and friends to fine-tune your messaging. Have a solid elevator pitch that clearly explains your idea in terms understandable to people outside of your field of expertise. The way you describe your idea will make a lot of sense to you, but don't assume it will make sense to others as well. Based on their feedback, you'll know if they are understanding your idea or not. If they are not, you should see this as a sign that you are not communicating it properly. You need to have a solid elevator pitch, as you never know when you'll need it.

And most importantly, follow your dreams. You won't know until you try, so don't let friends and family discourage you. The road won't be easy; it will be a lot of hard work, and at some point, you will either be ready to quit your day job and work even harder to build a company that you are excited about or you will realize you are not cut out for the grind and ups and downs of being an entrepreneur, which is fine. The end goal is to truly understand what makes you happy, and you won't figure it out by daydreaming. You are always one idea away from knowing.

Visit the below link for a chapter summary and resources related to this chapter.

www.ch5resources.sideadventure.com

CHAPTER 6

MANAGING PERSONAL FINANCES

"You must gain control over your money or
the lack of it will forever control you."
Dave Ramsey

"Don't tell me what you value, show me your
budget, and I'll tell you what you value."
Joe Biden

L earning how to manage your personal finances and
personal cash flow is extremely important, especially if
you want to pursue a side venture. After all, if you can't
manage your own finances, there is little chance you will be
successful in managing the finances of a side venture or early-
stage startup.

Most people learn about this topic the hard way. I sure
did. How money works, savings, compound interest, APR
(annual percentage rate), revenue, profit, margin, and fancier
accounting terms like EBITA (earnings before interest, taxes,
and amortization) are not things I learned about in high school
nor in college. After I graduated high school and was legally an
adult, credit card companies started flashing their offers in the
mail, through unsolicited calls, and booths at my college campus

offering gifts and rewards for applying for a credit card. Not fully understanding the impact of credit card debt and only being fed the importance of having a good credit score—which meant I needed to get multiple credit cards to build up my score—I applied for a few of these offers and got approved. The APRs were in the 25 percent range, but I didn't care. I didn't know any better. I also officially felt like an adult, as I had a couple of credit cards that had about a $2,000 spending limit.

I always had the intention to make a payment to have a zero balance at the end of the month, but it never worked that way. I had not established good financial habits and discipline. I also suffered from what I believe most young adults suffer from, which is a delusion in assuming you are young and you have a lot of time to pay off the credit card. After all, in just a few short years you are going to graduate and be making a lot of money, so having credit card debt is not an issue, right? It is if you are living as if you already have financial success long before you have that success.

The reality is that things can spiral out of control quickly, as they did for me. Before I knew it, I had about $10,000 in credit card debt. This might not sound like a big number, but back in the late 1990s and early 2000s, it was an excessively big number for me. To draw a comparison, minimum wage was $5.00 back in 1998. That is how much I was making at my fast food job. I did not come from a wealthy family and I watched my immigrant parents plant roots in a new country by relying on credit cards, which had ballooned into a large debt for them as well, so I could not ask them for help. On top of relying on payday advance check-cashing services, I also used student loans for non-education expenses, which was not a good idea either. Even though it was a relatively small student loan debt, it took me seventeen years to pay it off.

Once I graduated, the fancy high-paying job or the breakthrough project that would catapult me into a famous filmmaker was not there. Instead, whichever way I turned I was hearing crickets. I had to gain control of my life, so the first thing I did was educate myself about money and how people use money to generate wealth. It was an eye-opening educational experience. I then put having a good credit score aside and used a debt consolidation agency to help me come up with a plan to pay off my credit card debt. This resulted in a big drop in my credit score, but it didn't matter.

About a year later, I finally got what I considered a real job in the entertainment industry at one of the major studios. I was twenty-three years old and my income jumped from about $12,000 a year to $30,000 a year. Even though $30,000 is a small salary for today, I finally understood what financial freedom meant. Besides my debt consolidation payment, I had a small car payment and a cell phone bill, but no mortgage, no rent, and no utilities, as I was still living with my parents.

I promised myself that I would not be in that situation again, so with the extra income, I started investing part of it in the stock market. Fast forward about twelve years, and the regular investments into the stock market for over a decade— focusing on savings and not spending—turned into a large sum. This allowed us to purchase a fourth property with a large down payment, and to spend $150,000 on a complete remodel of the house. Even though I'm now in a position that I can instantly pay off a $10,000 credit card debt, I will not allow myself to get into long-term credit card debt. Excessive credit cards are similar to having a ball and chain attached to you wherever you go. It will slow you down in all aspects of your life.

What this experience taught me early on is that I need to manage my finances like a business. You have to act as the CFO of your own life and look at your income as revenue. The key is to figure out how much of your income is profit at the end of each month. Your profit will be in the form of savings and other investments. The higher percentage of your income you can maintain as profit, the faster you will generate wealth. This is called cash flow, and it is the key to managing your finances. Cash flow is knowing where every single dollar is coming from and where it is going.

In order to start your own side venture, you need to be successful at managing finances. Let's take a look at some key strategies that worked for me.

Do a deep analysis of your bank statements for the past six months. You will be surprised by what you discover with this simple exercise. This analysis will consist of putting each line item in your bank statement into a category so you can see how much you have coming in and going out at the category level. For example, categories will be: groceries, car, travel, eating out, shopping, gifts, etc. At the end of this chapter, I will provide some tools for you to use to do this.

With this analysis, the first thing you should do is minimize your expenses, especially your wasted expenses. If you are paying for live TV, Hulu, and Netflix, these are wasted expenses. Choose one and cancel the other two. What other monthly subscriptions do you have that you barely use? Cancel them. How much do you spend on eating out? If it is more than one dinner a week and more than two lunches a week, they are unnecessary expenses. Do you go into a grocery store to buy only what you need or do you drop products in your shopping cart that were not on your list? Supermarkets have been designed with years of research and analysis of human behavior. They know how to entice you to buy more than you need. You can save money each month if you get a better handle on this.

Audit your position. This means taking an analysis of your bank statements and layering on top how much you are making, your debt and how that debt is divided, your savings, and if you have money going into a long-term retirement fund—such as a 401K. Once you have a holistic view of your finances, you either need to eliminate your debt or consolidate your debt to reduce your monthly debt payments. Debt is the biggest blocker when trying to pursue a side venture, as it limits your financial freedom. An easy way to do this is by getting a debt consolidation loan, but you have to make sure you don't get this loan to then return to your habits of charging on the credit cards again. You have to have discipline, even if that means cutting up the cards so they are not at arm's reach.

Depending on the amount of your debt and your income, you might be able to pay off the debt if you have better cash flow. Do not enter the world of entrepreneurship with a lot of credit card debt. If you can't pay cash for that Vegas trip, then you can't go. If you gain traction on your side venture, your available personal credit might act as a boost to your side venture, which is another benefit of entering entrepreneurship with little to no credit card debt. Learning how to operate thin in your own life will pay off when you have to have lean operations in your side venture.

Obviously, if you are already debt-free and have large savings, the above is not for you. You have already mastered your finances, which is not the case for most. Based on research conducted in 2018 by Magnify Money, the average household savings in America is $16,420. The number drops to below $5,000 for the under forty-four-year-old age category. The rule of thumb is that you should be saving 20 percent of your income monthly. If you manage your expenses like a business, you can easily increase this number to 30 percent. If you get a bonus at the end of the year, over 50 percent of it should go into savings.

Savings are important, as you need to have an emergency fund. You need to be able to cover at least six months of your expenses if you decide to leave your job—we will talk about how to decide when to leave your job in a later chapter. You need another bucket of savings to be able to get your side venture started and to help you fund the prototype or even the MVP yourself as well as cover expenses for establishing the corporation, trademarks, or any other administrative expense that comes up when forming a company.

A crucial area that is often overlooked by the masses is taxes. Most people go about their year and pay taxes without really understanding the tax system and leave everything in the hands of an accountant or tax software. Tax planning should be part of your financial planning strategy. It starts by having an understanding of how the system works and how politicians impact the tax system. The wealthy use the system to their advantage. It's not always about making more money. It's also about how to keep more of it instead of paying Uncle Sam.

Even if you don't end up pursuing a side venture, by managing your personal cash flow better you can start enjoying and experiencing things you might have thought were reserved for the super-rich. While writing this book, we took our first vacation with our son Eric to Aulani in Hawaii. I also took my wife to Las Vegas for her birthday, where we had dinner at a Michelin-rated restaurant and enjoyed playing blackjack for hours—which just happens to be her favorite game and she is really good at it. For our five-year wedding anniversary, I surprised her with a private jet flight to Napa and dinner at French Laundry, a Michelin-rated restaurant that is roughly $400 per plate. We also went on a trip to Europe where we hopped from London to Paris to Brussels to Amsterdam. And yes, we did this while Eric was not even a year old. Call me crazy.

I'm not sharing this with you to brag, but rather to impress upon you that you can have similar experiences if you work hard, work up to a certain income level, and have really good cash-flow management. I think a household that earns $250,000 a year and has great cash flow management can easily experience some of the finer things in life without accumulating debt. The one thing you don't want to do is chase the Joneses. Don't get caught up in the game of comparing yourself to others. Otherwise, you will start living above your means and slowly increase your debt and be back at ground zero.

As you get a better handle on your personal cash flow, you also need to have a plan in place for the worst-case scenario. This is where insurance comes in. On top of health insurance—which most of you probably already have through your company—you should understand the different life insurance options. This protects your loved ones from tragic unforeseen events. The life insurance industry has developed many products, so educate yourself before making a purchase. In addition, you should have disability insurance to protect yourself in case you are not able to work. There are also various types of disability insurance, both offered through your employer and independent companies, so educate yourself before making a purchase.

You might now be asking yourself: This all makes sense, but is there a system or best practice that I can use to help me manage my cash flow better? I'm going to share with you exactly what I have done for years that has worked well for me. You can adopt my system or modify and improve it for your personal situation.

Whether you are single or married, there is a paycheck that you are getting on a regular basis. Write down what your take-home is. If you are contributing to a 401K or any other type of retirement fund, split your take-home into take-home cash and retirement.

Next, write down all your fixed monthly bills not related to your house, condo, or apartment—cell phone, student loan, car insurance, etc. Add all of these monthly expenses and subtract it from your take-home cash. This new number is now the cash you have available monthly.

Then, make a list of your credit card debt and your monthly payments. Hopefully you are debt-free or have very little debt. If you feel your credit card debt is out of control, you should seek out a debt consolidation expert or a bankruptcy lawyer so you can get educated on your options. Add up all your credit card payments and subtract it from your free cash flow available to you after your fixed monthly payments.

Let's add up your living expenses. Rent or mortgage, utilities, cable and internet, groceries, and other house expenses. If you own a house, you probably have additional expenses but you don't have an HOA payment, unless your house is part of a private community. I highly encourage you to pay yourself a small monthly HOA. Maintenance and repair costs always come up and this is a good way to plan for it.

Subtract your living expenses from the updated cash flow you came up with after your credit card payment. Now you have your true cash flow number. Experts say that 20 percent of your take-home should go into savings. I would go higher if possible but if not, go down to 10 percent. After putting money aside for savings, this new number is the amount of cash flow you have on a monthly basis for your personal expenses and leisure. If the number is shocking, you have a lot of work to do before you can pursue a side venture.

Now you know exactly how much money is needed for each bucket described above each month. Depending on how many paychecks you get a month—usually four or two—divide the total from each of the categories by two or four. This will give you the breakdown of how each of your paychecks cover these expenses.

The system to manage all of this money going in and out is multiple bank accounts. You need a bank account for your house expenses, an account for your fixed monthly payments, an account for your credit card payments, and an account for your personal spending. If you are married or have a partner you share expenses with, both of you need your own personal spending account, and you need to calculate the categories I mentioned above using both of your pay.

Assuming most of you have direct deposit, now that you know how each paycheck breaks down into the various categories, you should have your pay automatically divided into the respective bank accounts. Be disciplined enough not to touch the funds in the non-personal expenses account and only use the funds you have in your personal expenses account for daily expenses and leisure. If the amount seems too small, then you are either living above your means or have too much debt and have to get a handle on your expenses. If the calculation described above sounds too complicated, don't worry. Use the link below to use the tool I created to make this easy for you.

Finally, I'm not an accountant, CPA, or financial advisor and I'm only sharing with you what worked for me. For professional advice, please contact a financial expert, as they will be able to provide personalized advice and help you find potential blind spots.

Visit the below link for a chapter summary and resources related to this chapter.

www.ch6resources.sideadventure.com

CHAPTER 7

I HAVE A GREAT IDEA. NOW WHAT?

"Ideas Won't Keep. Something Must Be Done About Them." Alfred North Whitehead

"There Is One Thing Stronger Than All the Armies in The World, And That Is an Idea Whose Time Has Come." Victor Hugo

---

As far back as I can remember, I have always enjoyed the process of coming up with an idea and, even more so, sharing that idea with others—and hopefully receive positive feedback, which fed my brain lies that most of my ideas are good. This is usually what happens when you come up with an idea and, without doing much leg work, share that idea with friends and family, who are going to tell you it's a good idea, not because they are lying, but because they truly believe it is. That is because most people have not learned the process of validating an idea.

This simple skill gap has led to many people pursuing ideas that never had a chance, which led to a lot of wasted time and money. I'm guilty of it as well. Looking back, my initial few attempts to build a software product were a failure not because I did not know what I was doing, which was also true, but because the ideas were not good. The advice "fail quickly" comes from the idea that failing is how you learn the skill of validating an idea. Failing is the path most people take to acquire this skill, but I want you to learn from my failures so you can fast track to the truly good idea. You are one idea away from success.

Don't romanticize too early about your idea being a unicorn and all the fame and fortune that comes with it. The word unicorn is used to describe startups that are valued at more than $1 billion, and there aren't many of them compared to the number of startups. You should think big, but start small and scale quickly once you have product market fit.

It is a regular occurrence that someone comes to me with an idea and asks me what I think. Nine out of ten times, I can tell immediately whether they have thought about the idea after that initial spark. That is because the first mental shift you need to make is not to look for ideas, but to look for problems. Ask yourself: What problem does the idea solve?

Many new entrepreneurs get stuck on the product and the features and in many cases chasing the next feature, thinking that the next feature is what will cause customers and users to flock to the product. I made this mistake multiple times and it cost me a lot of time and money. We would come up with a great feature idea or hear of a great feature idea from whom we had identified as potential customers and we would dive in right away to design, develop, and deploy that feature. We were never clear on the problem we were trying to solve, so no matter how many great features we threw at it, the product never gained traction.

Don't ever assume that, "if you build it, they will come." Write down the problem your idea is solving and let this statement be the guiding light that takes you to the next steps. Asking the following questions can help you identify problems:

- Why does something cost so much? Having the curiosity to actually dig into this might uncover a problem that may be the foundation of a new business.

- Can technology be used to cut out the middleman? This is what technology is good at—when was the last time you used a travel agent?

- Why does it take so long to do this certain thing?

- Can a solution work in multiple industries? Uber and Airbnb kicked off the sharing economy and that model is now used for Cars by Turo and in other industries.

- Why does this product or service frustrate me? If you are frustrated by a product or service, chances are you are not alone.

Let's use Uber as an example. The founders of Uber were seasoned and successful entrepreneurs, so they did not necessarily start with an idea. They observed a problem: San Francisco's taxi industry. For anyone who has been in a taxi before, it's never been a great experience, but customers did not have a choice. The story goes that one of the founders was watching Casino Royale. There is a scene where James Bond uses his cell phone to find a car. That is what brought them to launch Uber.

Now that you have the problem written down, if your idea, which might soon be a product, solves this problem, what kind of value does it bring to the users and customers? Does their life change for the better? Can they do something faster and cheaper? Using Uber again as an example, the value of Uber is a safer, more transparent, and more convenient way to catch a ride—certainly much better than a taxi. It also provides value for the drivers and the jobs it has created. This is called the value proposition. You will wordsmith this many times once you are actually building the product as the value proposition. This is what visitors to your landing and marketing pages should see. For now, having a sense of the value proposition is good enough to help you validate your idea, as your solution might change and evolve over time. This is called a "pivot." Many startups go through this step when trying to find product market fit. Product market fit is when your product or service has satisfied your addressable market and has met their demand.

As an example, Instagram started as a product called Burbn, which was intended to be a location-based, check-in app focused on photos, similar to Foursquare. Once the founders realized that most of its early users were only using the photo-related features in the app, especially the filters, they pivoted to a new product called Instagram. This is also a great example of why your product needs to do one thing and do it extremely well. We will get into this in more detail in a future chapter.

The next question you need to ask yourself is: Who is your customer or end user? You need to be very specific—so simply saying "Millennials" won't cut it. Getting specific is important because it will help you find the early potential users of the product to get feedback. If possible, you should write a hypothetical customer profile. This is your demographic. Now that you know what your customer looks like, you know how big your market is, both from the perspective of users or customers and how much money is spent by customers in the industry you are targeting.

Understanding your market is crucial. You need to make sure you are solving a problem that is large enough to sustain a profitable business. This is also referred to as your addressable market. At this point in your market research, you also need to identify who your competition might be to gauge your barrier to entry. If your idea solves problems related to ride-sharing, no matter how novel your idea might be, the barrier to entry will be extremely high, so it's probably not an idea worth pursuing at this time.

Market research and competitive analysis are a key part of validating your idea. Don't waste your time and money if your idea is not unique and does not solve a large enough problem. Competition will make it hard to break through, especially if you will need to rely on a network effect to be successful. Uber would not have worked in its early days if it did not have thousands of drivers and even more riders. Facebook would not have worked if enough of your friends were not on the platform. This is called a network effect.

By going through the above process, you will have better clarity on your idea and the problem you are trying to solve, who your potential users and customers are, who the competition might be, and the size of your addressable market. If you still believe the idea is worth pursuing, your next step is to validate the idea with potential customers or users.

There are two easy and low-cost ways to do this. The first approach is using social media—LinkedIn, Facebook, Instagram, and Twitter—to reach at least two hundred people that fit your demographic. You should approach them as a mentee asking a mentor (the potential customer) for feedback and advice. To do this you need to be able to describe your future product, what problem it is solving, and the benefits in a short and crisp message. This is essentially your marketing copy, which will end up living on your landing pages in various permutations.

A reach-out message format that I have found effective starts with a brief introduction of who you are and then emphasizing that you believe they are an expert in the field so you want their advice and feedback. You want to start with this to eliminate the possibility of the reader thinking your message is some kind of spam sales message. Next, you need to describe the problem you have observed. This lets the reader know you are knowledgeable about the space. Don't oversell yourself, as you don't want to come across as a know-it-all. Chances are the person you are writing to knows a lot more about the industry than you do. Stay humble. Then explain your product idea, the benefits, and how it aims to solve the problem you believe they have. Ask them if they think the problem you describe is really a problem for them and if it is, would they use a product that offers the benefits you described. End it with a thank you and how grateful you are for feedback and advice. This entire message should be no longer than five or six sentences—people are busy and will not read long messages from a person they do not know.

Do not be discouraged if you do not get many responses. This is normal, and it is why you want to target at least 200 people so you can get about twenty or twenty-five replies. If the majority of people respond by agreeing with your problem statement and they like your solution, then you are on to something and are ready to build a prototype to further test your solution and gather more feedback and data.

A second approach to validating your idea is by setting up a temporary homepage/landing page for your product. You can do this using Wix, WordPress, Squarespace, or various other drag and drop website builders available in the market or services that specialize in setting up landing pages—I will provide you with a list at the end of this chapter. You can also ask a friend or colleague for help if they know how to build webpages. I have found Wix to be the easiest one for me to use, as I'm in full control and the features and options I need are all available.

You will need a domain address. Don't get caught up on registering the perfect domain name if you don't already own something you can use. Use GoDaddy to register a name that sounds like a good representation of the company to make the landing page look believable—this approach will take longer not only because you have to have a good name for your product, but you also need basic product photos. This is doable, as there are many templates in the marketplace. The companies I have used for design templates are Graphicriver, Themeforest, Wix, Squarespace, and Templatemonster. It takes some time and effort to do your research and find the right templates, but it is a crucial step that you need to focus on. Don't worry about a logo at this stage, just use a template.

The goal is to create a professional product homepage that allows a visitor to provide an email address to join a mailing list for updates or request a demo. Obviously, there is no product to demo yet, so the ultimate goal is to see how much interest there is in the product. The minimum conversion rate you should have is 5 percent. Ideally, you want to shoot for 10 percent and higher. If you're not getting at least 5 percent of visitors taking action, then you're not driving the right traffic to your page, you haven't perfected your marketing copy, or your marketing copy is sharp but visitors don't need your solution.

You have now set up your homepage, but how do you get people to visit it? The most effective approach I have found is social media advertising. You will need to do some reading on the steps to launch social media ads on various platforms. I have some suggested reading at the end of this chapter to help you but, assuming you know the tactical steps in creating ads, using your marketing copy, you will draft multiple versions to use as your ad copy. Using websites like iStockphoto, Shutterstock, or other websites that offer royalty-free photos and images, you will find images that are representative of your product as if you had done a custom photoshoot or design and used them for the ads.

The reason you want to run multiple ads with various photos and images is that digital ads also allow you to test what kind of imagery and copy resonates with your target demographic. This will be valuable information when you move to the next step—building your prototype. Establish a budget for these ads and let them fly. Now sit back and analyze the data. If the results are not positive, change the ads. If you are getting very little response to your ads or people are clicking through to your landing page but not providing an email, this is probably a sign that you should not pursue your idea.

If using one or both of these approaches yields positive feedback, you need to validate the technology needed to build your solution. If you can't build your solution using existing tools and programming language, it will be difficult for you to move forward, as you are not in a position to fund research and development. If you can build your solution with existing tools and programming languages, you can move forward, but this does not mean you are ready for a big launch party. Validating an idea is an iterative process, and at each step, you are trying to collect data to inform your next step. There will be more bad ideas than great ideas but remember, you are one idea away from finding something you can be passionate about.

Visit the below link for a chapter summary and resources related to this chapter.

www.ch7resources.sideadventure.com

CHAPTER 8

FORMING A COMPANY

"The way to get started is to quit talking and
begin doing."
Walt Disney

"With so many demands on your time, one of
the areas that often slips through the cracks is
establishing a solid legal foundation for your
company. Although there is no set amount
of time, energy, and money a company
should spend on legal early on, if you're
operating in a heavily regulated area—such
as crowdfunding, payments, or health care—
you'll want to focus more on legal than if
you're creating the next Candy Crush."
Matt Glick

As this chapter is about legal entities and legal agreements,
you should consult with your attorney and tax
professional. Everyone's scenario is unique and I'm
neither an attorney nor a tax professional, but I want to offer you
a broad understanding of your options and considerations so
you are more educated and informed.

When I was in the process of starting my first failed side
venture attempt, I knew I should form a company but was

uneducated on the options. Mistakes were made. Luckily, depending on how you look at it, the venture failed so the mistakes I made in how the company was formed and the legal agreements that we had or did not have did not matter. Since you are going to leverage my fails and learnings to give you a higher chance of success, you should make fewer mistakes in how you establish your side venture as a legal entity, how you think about equity, and what you include in your partner agreement, if you decide to have a partner join you on this adventure.

One of the first mistakes first-time entrepreneurs make is either not forming a legal company or forming a company without consulting a lawyer and tax professional. This usually leads to higher taxes and being personally subject to liabilities that could have easily been avoided. There is a minor cost to forming a company, and at an early stage, my go-to is Legal Zoom. It provides a low-cost option but does not replace discussing your specific needs and considerations with an attorney. The benefits far outweighed the cost.

When you form a company, there is a credibility factor that comes with having an Inc., LLC, or whatever designation is given to legal companies in your country. In addition, if you are going to raise funds, legally forming a company is a requirement. Whether you got money from friends and family, an Angel investor, or professional investment from a Venture Capital (VC), they are buying equity in your company that has some legal oversight from the Federal Exchange Commission (FEC), or equivalent of the FEC in your country, even though your company is not publicly traded—you can only do this with a legally formed entity.

As you begin building the actual product, your company name, logos, and any intellectual property (IP) should become trademarks, patents, and copyrights that give your company value. Investors will want to see all IP legally assigned to your company. Failure to do this can negatively impact future investments, as ownership might be grey, turning into a risk an investor is not willing to take.

Most importantly, a legally formed company will protect you from being personally liable if the company gets tangled up in a legal suit with other shareholders, customers, employees, or investors. If you have decided to bring on a cofounder, one of your first agreements will be your partner agreement. After that, you will enter into agreements with vendors, contractors, and hopefully employees and investors. A breach of these agreements will in most cases protect you and the company directors from personal claims. In reverse, if you are being sued by a creditor, the creditor cannot go after you to recoup debt. This mitigation of risk for the company directors and founders, and for the company, is something any investor will want to see before they commit to writing you a check.

Now that you understand why forming a company is a must, let's talk about the different entity options. The following section is focused on US entities, so please do your own reading and consult a professional to understand the various entity options in your country.

The two most simple types of companies are sole proprietorships and general partnerships. These two require little legal documentation and fees except for picking a unique name and registering the Doing Business As (DBA). The problem with these two types of companies is that they do not offer the benefits I talked about, so they should not be considered. If for any reason you have gone down this route, mainly because you wanted to quickly register and protect your company name, know that you can always convert a sole proprietorship and general partnership into one of the other types of companies.

You are now left with three viable options when forming a company. The first one is a Limited Liability Company

(LLC). An LLC incorporates elements from the other types of companies. The owners or shareholders of an LLC are known as members, and the members that are operating the company are known as managing members. There is no limit on the number of members an LLC can have. The LLC provides its officers, members, and investors the protection of not being personally liable and, when it comes to taxes, the IRS and the state pass down gains and losses to your personal tax return while there is a flat tax you pay at the state level. For example, this fee is $800 in California. LLCs are governed by state law, so you should check with your state on the specific rules and regulations.

There are some key items I want you to be aware of. Some states require an LLC to have at least two members. Members are compensated using either distribution of profit or guaranteed payments, but the most important point is that if you are going to raise VC money, have a large number of shareholders, or are successful enough to go public, an LLC is not a good model. So, if you do start off as an LLC, know that at some point you will have to convert your company into a C-Corp. Also, an LLC cannot issue stock, but each member receives units, and the member's role in an LLC is governed by the partnership agreement, which does give an LLC flexibility in dictating certain voting rights. Once you are a member of an LLC, your membership (or ownership) cannot be freely transferred to someone else unless there is specific language in the membership agreement. In most cases, transfer of membership requires approval from other members.

Your second option is an S-Corp, which provides similar liability protection for its managers and shareholders as an LLC. In addition, an S-Corp is taxed similar to an LLC where profits are passed through to its shareholders and managers to be taxed at their personal income tax level with an advantage for tax savings for what is considered excess profits. As an example, a

$100,000 profit in an LLC will get hit with all the various taxes at your personal income tax level. The same $100,000 profit under an S-Corp can be treated as $50,000 of salary—which gets hit with all the various taxes—and the other $50,000 can be considered business profits and will not be subject to taxes that are for individuals, like social security tax.

However, an S-Corp is limited to 100 shareholders. This might not be an issue right now, but as the number of employees that are eligible for stock options and the number of investors grows, this limitation can become an issue. S-Corps generally have more stringent rules than an LLC. One of the most important rules is its limitation to only have one class of stock, meaning all shareholders have the same voting rights. This is important to understand, as you and your cofounder might want to maintain voting control over the company at the early stage. With an LLC you can stipulate that you and your cofounder have the voting units while your early investors and early employees have units that have limited or no voting power, but you cannot do this with an S-Corp. This of course comes down to your negotiations with your investor and employees, as you might have to give them the same voting rights at an early stage in the company to get them on board. Unlike an LLC, stocks owned in an S-Corp can be transferred to others if IRS requirements are met. Generally, S-Corps cannot own another S-Corp or LLC, so if you want to form multiple companies to be owned by a parent company, an LLC and C-Corp would allow this to happen, but not an S-Corp.

Your third option is a C-Corp. Almost all corporations and publicly traded companies are C-Corp. Usually, a startup begins as an LLC or an S-Corp, then converts to a C-Corp when necessary. A C-Corp is a much more complex type of entity that requires more paperwork and more expense to set up and manage. There is also the potential for double taxation—however, it does allow for more tax benefits. If you are raising more than five million dollars, professional investors want the company to be a C-Corp, as it allows more flexibility and strategy options in how ownership is defined. Unlike an S-Corp, C-Corps can have an unlimited number of shareholders, which is why all publicly traded companies are C-Corps. Besides the differences in taxes and no restrictions on shareholders and ownership that an S-Corp has, another big difference between a C-Corp, LLC, and S-Corp is that foreigners can have stock in a C-Corp while LLC members, and the max 100 shareholders of an S-Corp, must be US citizens.

Depending on the situation, I have formed both LLCs and S-Corps when initially establishing a legal entity for my side ventures. One of the strategies you should pay close attention to is your tax strategy. As noted above, with LLCs and S-Corps, profits are passed through and taxed at the individual level, which also means that losses are passed through—most likely, the first couple of years you will show losses.

As you continue working at your corporate job, you are paying taxes on every paycheck. Adding on the losses of your side venture to your income tax will mean that you will see a higher tax return the following year, which you can re-invest into your side venture. Another tax strategy is more forward-looking, which you can use to plan when you might want to get started with your side venture. As an example, if you are single and making $110,000, you are in the 24 percent federal tax bracket and you will owe the IRS roughly $17,000. The 22 percent bracket caps at $84,199 so if you can show $26,000 in losses from your side venture, not only are you now obligated to pay taxes on $84,000 of taxable income, you are also now in a lower bracket. If you have been paying taxes per paycheck based on $110,000 taxable income but filing taxes and showing $84,000 as taxable income, you will now be getting a refund of the taxes you have been paying during the year. Even though this is your money, it does feel like finding money, which you can re-invest into the business or use to start a new one. But be careful with this strategy, as certain things—such as buying a house—require your tax return, and even though you can afford the house, your tax return might be telling another story and banks will not approve you for a high enough loan.

The last thing to consider after deciding the type of entity you want to form is where you will actually register the company. Most people's default is to register the company in your home state. This might be a good idea for LLCs in some states, but do your due diligence and consult an attorney before you jump the gun. Your other option is to register in Delaware, as the state has business-friendly laws, which is why most startups start as being registered in Delaware and most seasoned investors expect a startup to be registered in Delaware.

Once you have your company legally registered, the two most important agreements you will need are your operating agreement and your founder's agreement. A founder's agreement outlines the roles and responsibilities of the founders and owners in the company in addition to outlining various what-if scenarios to prevent or minimize future conflict. This agreement tries to also address equity-related questions when partners enter or exit the business on top of acting as a skeleton version of your business plan—it shows investors that you are serious. This can be a separate agreement or embedded within the operating agreement of an LLC.

If you are starting your venture with a cofounder, do not overlook having a legally binding agreement, even if your cofounder is your best friend or your sibling and you think you will work things out. As always, consult an attorney for the best advice and guidance for your situation. All I want to do is introduce you to some key points that you will have to consider when working on your founder's agreement.

We will discuss partnerships in a future chapter, but most of what you agree on should find itself in your founder's agreement. This starts by describing what the company is and your goals, vision, and intention for the company. In most cases, your goals and intentions will change over time, which is OK. You can have a clause in your agreement that allows for the agreement to be amended as often as you and your cofounders agree, but it is very important to agree and document what each founder's roles and responsibilities will be at this early formation stage of the company. Not only will this help provide guidance and avoid confusion, it also will streamline decision-making and form more efficient operations focused on your shared vision and goal. Thinking that every founder should be involved in every decision is a bad approach because it will slow down the project and create tension that can be detrimental to the company.

You then want to get specific on how the side venture is being funded to get it off the ground—kudos to you if you already have an investor. Know that you will need an investor's agreement as well but, in most cases, a side venture for first-time entrepreneurs will be funded by the cofounders to get it off the ground. It also goes without saying that you will need more funding at some point to continue. It is a good idea to address how founders will continue to fund the company and the impact this has on equity.

The next important section in your agreement deals with equity. Something to consider when trying to figure out equity splits is capital investment: Is one cofounder contributing more capital than the other? Besides capital, is someone bringing something of value to the company at the formation stage? Maybe a patent or a prototype? How much time will each person commit to the project? If you are semi full-time because you still have your corporate job but your cofounder can dedicate himself full time to the venture, his or her time should equate to more equity. If your cofounder is an established entrepreneur with contacts and relationships, they will most likely request more equity. Also, roles and responsibilities should play a part in this equation, as whoever wears the CEO hat usually has slightly more equity than other C-suite-level roles.

Once you have figured out how equity is being split, you should consider having a vesting schedule. This places restrictions on the founder's ability to sell or transfer the stock or membership to others. For example, a vesting schedule can protect the company if a cofounder has 40 percent equity and decides to leave the company three months after they joined. In this case, the 40 percent will revert to the company where the agreement should outline how this situation will be handled. The most common vesting schedule is a four-year vesting schedule where, at the end of each twelve-month period, the cofounder has earned 25 percent of their total equity and can do what he/she wants with it according to your agreement and state and federal law. If a cofounder decides to sell their vested shares, a common clause in an agreement is the "right of first refusal" clause, which gives the company first choice in buying back the stocks or units. Be careful, as this will impact your valuation. Investors will use the last sale of stock or unit to value your company, which can result in you not being able to raise enough funds or having to give up more of the company than you want.

Documenting how much equity you want to put in a separate bucket to reward future employees is important at this stage. You will not be able to compete based on salary, so offering equity is how you can attract talent that believes in the company you are building and is willing to risk less immediate pay to have small ownership of a company that hopefully becomes a multi-million—or in rare instances, a unicorn—company.

There are various ways you can award equity to early employees. First-time entrepreneurs that have not done their due diligence default to issuing equity in the form of a certain percentage in the company. The problem with this method is that you will run out of the equity available to assign. Let's say you want to give your first twenty employees equity. You can't give them 1 percent each, as that means you have just handed out 20 percent of your company. If you use fractions—such as .25 percent—it no longer sounds enticing enough for a potential employee to take the risk and join you on your journey.

A better way to issue equity to early employees is through shares or units. Let's say you formed your company with ten million shares or units. Reserving 5 percent of the company for employee equity means five hundred thousand shares/units are now reserved. Giving early employees twenty-five thousand shares/units sounds more enticing and exciting, as it is easy to do best-case-scenario math. If investors end up paying $20 a share to invest in the company, that employee's shares are now worth $500,000 on paper—I say on paper because you should never just hand out all of the equity on day one.

There are various ways you can issue shares. One approach is to issue restricted stock, meaning the stock they have been issued is not technically theirs until certain restrictions and criteria are met. For example, say you have hired a director of growth. The criteria for this employee to earn his/her shares might be that they must hit a certain user acquisition number by a certain date. The other method is a vesting schedule similar to what you and your cofounder have agreed to. Discuss these and other options available to you with your attorney.

An important thing to understand when it comes to equity is dilution. This is when the company has to issue more stock because of funding or add more stock to the employee pool. This means that as you issue more stock, the percentage of the company people own goes down, but the number of shares they own stays the same. Using the same ten million share example, if an investor funds the company in exchange for 25 percent of the company, they are not getting 2,500,000 shares from the ten million. You will have to issue 3,300,000 new shares, taking the total shares to 13,300,000. If you previously had 55 percent of the company because you owned 5,500,000 shares, you still own 5,500,000 shares but your percentage ownership has now dropped to 41 percent. Do not look at this negatively. You need to view ownership more in terms of dollars and voting rights. Your 55 percent ownership might have been worth $550,000 on paper but with the funding you just received, your 41 percent might now be worth $1,320,000 because the funding resulted in the value of your company going up on paper.

As you begin building your product, you are building IP. Your founder's agreement must cover IP to ensure anything produced, patents, trademarks, copyrights, and any trade secrets remain the property of the company and not the individual that worked on it. This is an extremely vital point, and it extends to anyone within the company or associated with the company that is contributing to the building of the product, the brand, and the company. If any IP was produced before the company was legally formed, you need to make sure all of this IP is assigned to the company as well to prevent any issues down the line.

One of the more complicated sections of a founder's agreement is the voluntary resignation or the involuntary removal of a founder from the company, typically referred to as the Exit Clause. There are many things to consider here, depending on the maturity of the company. Don't overlook this section and always consult your attorney. This will help avoid a lot of potential drama and keep the focus on what really matters.

It is important to start your company on good legal grounds, as it sets up the foundation for many things to come. Hopefully this chapter has given you a basic understanding of the various legal entities and important sections to consider in an agreement, and highlighted the importance of consulting your attorney and accountant for professional advice that is specific to your needs and situation.

Visit the below link for a chapter summary and resources related to this chapter.

www.ch8resources.sideadventure.com

CHAPTER 9

DO I NEED A COFOUNDER?

"Founder is a state of mind, not a job description, and if done right, even CEOs who join after day 1 can become founders." Reid Hoffman

"Discussing issues with your cofounder could get uncomfortable, create rifts, or even uncover deal-breakers. If you are able to successfully have these difficult conversations, this is a testament to your partnership and to the strength of your relationship—and will serve as a solid foundation from which to grow your business." David Ehrenberg

As discussed in the previous chapter, it is wise to establish a solid legal foundation before starting product development. This is also the stage to ponder the idea of a cofounder.

I was lucky to have Michael as a friend. We had already collaborated on a few films and entrepreneurial projects and we had a solid working relationship. We had similar drives, interests, and philosophies but also complementary skills and, to this day, we bounce ideas off each other.

One of our earlier software product collaborations was a service that would allow you to send anonymous emails using predefined templates to avoid hate mail and other types of harassment. Today, some services allow you to do this, but back then—the pre-App Store days—we were trying to solve a personal problem. We wanted to tell our bosses how wrong they were. As a product, it wasn't a good idea. We were new to the entrepreneurial world, so we thought we had a brilliant idea and spent our own money and time building it. We did not follow any of the steps I have outlined in the previous chapters, and you can imagine it was a failure from the start.

We had another idea during the same time period: making the car-buying experience much easier and transparent. This idea was born from my own frustrating car-buying experiences. This time, we probably had a good idea and a large enough problem to build a business around. Think of services available today like TrueCar, Carvana, Vroom, and Shift. To put things into perspective, Carvana went public in 2017 and, at the time of writing this chapter, they are valued at twelve billion dollars. Maybe this could have been our company years before, but our execution was nonexistent—we had no experience.

When my time came to ponder a cofounder, my choice was easy. I knew I wanted Michael as my cofounder. Just like any relationship, communication and setting and agreeing on expectations is key in a cofounder relationship. For the last project that we started together, Michael had to step away after about a year, which was fine, as we had everything in place for this to happen with zero impact to our friendship and the startup. I have also tried to bring others on board to side ventures as cofounders, which didn't work out, so I have experienced the good and the bad. Having said that, a cofounder is not a must, and there are things you should be aware of.

You have probably heard of the legendary cofounders Steve Jobs and and Steve Wozniack, or Bill Gates and Paul Allen, but you have also heard of solo founders Jeff Bezos and Mark Zuckerberg. It's hard to say which route is better—solo or with cofounders—but the general consensus and advice is that you need to build a great team. This is why many investors and accelerator programs mainly fund startups with multiple cofounders, as they are investing in the people as much as the product and company.

You probably do not have the bandwidth or the skills to do everything, and you do not have the funds yet to hire a team, so a cofounder with complementary skills, passion for the project, and similar vision would be the right choice. But what if you do not know anyone that matches these criteria? This is OK, as a cofounder can enter a project at any time. It does not mean you are setting up your MVP for failure.

A recent study based on the data from CrunchBase found that, of the companies that have raised less than $10 million in funding, 46 percent were single founders and 32 percent had two founders. In addition, thousands of companies that had reported some kind of exit, which means the founders sold or left the company, were analyzed and from these companies, 53 percent were single founders and 30 percent had two founders. I don't share this data with you to push you to be a solo founder, but to show you people have had success as solo founders, so if you need to delay getting a cofounder it's OK. Even though starting and running a startup is extremely difficult and stressful, especially if this is your first side venture, having a cofounder does have its advantages.

A cofounder will share responsibilities. At this stage, you are still employed, so having to do everything on your own is not only overwhelming but will dramatically slow you down. Getting to market fast is critical. The initial stages of building a product and a company are also stressful, so to have someone that can help with lowering the stress level and can relate makes a difference.

Michael and I would talk to each other daily about the last side venture we worked on together. Hearing each other's updates was motivation because if one of us had completed our to-do list, it forced the other one not to fall behind, and being able to ask each other for help made the process feel more enjoyable and real, as we could visualize success together. It is easy to talk yourself out of going to the gym, but not as easy when you've hired a personal trainer. Having a cofounder increases your personal accountability level, as you do not want to disappoint each other, which ends up being a great thing for the product and company you are building.

Having a cofounder that has complementary skills will increase the odds of success. You might have a sales or marketing background, but how are you going to operate the business with no operational experience? That is where a cofounder with an operational background will be able to move things much faster than you can. If you're reading this book, you are most likely not an engineer, so the best cofounder you can find is someone who can bring some technical experience and expertise into the project and will not only increase your learning curve, but they might be able to do some of the coding themselves, which will save you money and time as well. Different backgrounds also bring different viewpoints, thus you may be able to tackle problems from different angles. A cofounder will also provide a different network to tap into for help and hopefully future employees or advisors. Diverse ideas will close gaps and help you look and be better.

Having someone constructively challenge your ideas will lead to better decision-making. You might have suggestions for a company name, marketing copy, how a feature should work, or the millions of other big and small decisions that need to be made. Brainstorming with a good cofounder will make good ideas great and filter out the bad ones.

Back in the mid-2000s, Michael and I were working for a major studio and our offices were doors apart. Multiple times throughout the day, we would get together and, with enthusiasm and passion, share what we thought was the next great idea. Both of us would get so passionate about the concept that at some point during the conversation, getting the other to like it would trump the idea itself. We would debate our position and Google data to try to prove a point but eventually, in most cases, we would both bring the other down to earth, as the ideas weren't that good. A healthy relationship with your cofounder will do the same for you.

Having a cofounder will help you mitigate risks. There will be costs involved to build a prototype and the MVP, and having someone to share these costs with will reduce the stress and anxiety. It also mitigates risks for investors. As a solo founder, what if circumstances change for you and you need to exit the project? You are the heart of the company, so leaving will have a negative impact. A cofounder gives investors, who are already taking a huge risk by investing in a seed round—at the very early stage of a startup—peace of mind that a founder leaving the project doesn't also mean a loss of their investment. No matter how much you think you know about all the skills needed to build a successful startup, you will have huge knowledge gaps in many areas. A cofounder also helps you mitigate this risk by reducing the knowledge gap.

You are probably thinking that you'd rather be in full control, you want your vision to come true and the spotlight all on you. Unless you are a serial entrepreneur having built multiple multi-million- or billion-dollar companies, I need to stop you right now and let you know that you are thinking with your ego and, unless you become humble willingly, the ruthless business world will humble you and your fantasies will stay as that. After all, owning part of something that has value is better than owning all of something that has no value.

In most cases, having a cofounder happens in three ways. One way is when multiple people are involved in the ideation process and then form a partnership to execute. This partnership can be in the form of two people sharing responsibilities or it can be one person committing all their time to executing the idea while a second person provides the funding. A second way is when a single person has taken the idea as far as they could and have some traction and funding and they hire a cofounder to help take the company to the next level. A third way is when you are part of an accelerator program or have an Angel investor where, in both cases, the terms of them investing in your company include them picking a cofounder to complement your skills and experience because they perceive you are lacking as a solo founder.

You might not have enough traction yet to attract investors and cofounders. You probably don't have previous success to ride on to raise funds and you are not in a place yet to quit your job to pursue your side venture full-time. If you started your side venture with a partner that is either committing time or money, you are slightly ahead, but the rest of this chapter should still be relevant.

You will find that a friend, family member, or coworker is the only cofounder you are able to attract at this stage. This is not a bad thing. You already know which of your friends, family members, or coworkers you can trust and that have the necessary skills and experience to go on this journey with you. You know who might share the same passion, drive, and work ethic as you, but before you start pitching, there are some key points you need to understand and consider.

Most importantly, just like investors, your friends, family members, and coworkers will want to see some traction. Pitch to family and friends when your prototype is built. Everyone hears ideas on a daily basis, and most go up in smoke, so you need to convince the candidates that have known you for years that you are not all talk. Impress them with your prototype and a professional pitch deck to show them you are serious and have done your due diligence. No matter how long you have known these people and how perfect your relationship is with them, they are going to qualify you based on the work you have put in thus far. This is a business relationship they are pondering to enter, and they need to assess if they will be wasting their time and money on you or if you potentially have something special. At the same time, you need to further qualify your candidates, as you might need to know more about them to decide if you want them as a cofounder.

The person you choose must be passionate. You are probably asking yourself how to quantify if a person is passionate about a startup trying to connect users with mobile car wash services. First of all, your pitch should be purpose-driven, as you need to sell benefits and emotions—not the actual product. But when I say your cofounder needs to be passionate, I do not mean passionate about what you are trying to build. Your cofounder needs to be passionate about life and want to do big things to not only win for their family but leave some kind of legacy and leave this planet slightly better. This type of person will be able to overcome obstacles and challenges and not quit in the face of adversity, as that passion and obsession for winning is too strong to hold them back. They have set a much higher bar for themselves than most. This is the person you want in your corner. If you settle for a person who is not as driven as you are, your venture will suffer.

Just like in any other type of successful relationship, trust is pivotal when working together. You will be in stressful situations, meeting many new people, hiring people, tackling projects together and independently under the guides of the same goal, and, if you're fortunate, having to handle a lot of money, so you need someone you can trust with your company.

Having an open and honest line of communication is equally important. If your potential cofounder is in a relationship, are they looking to get married soon? Are they able to work early morning and at night? What do they like and not like? You need to be aware of their priorities and where on the list the side venture falls. I made this mistake once, of assuming that my cofounder considered our side venture to be a top priority as I did, which resulted in me falling behind on schedule and having to let go of the cofounder. Communication will help reduce friction when stress level and pressure is high. You also need to be on the same page on the vision, mission, and goals of the side venture. If your vision changes along the way, it's important that your cofounder is on board as well.

A cofounder should complement your skills and personality, not be exactly like you. Take an honest assessment of your skills and personality type—I have provided some links at the end of this chapter to help you. If you are the builder and introverted type who doesn't like to speak in public, your cofounder should be the marketing and extroverted type who can eloquently and confidently drive a presentation. If you find a cofounder that is just like you, the outcome will probably be a great product that neither of you are good at marketing and selling. I'm a believer that anyone can learn any skill they want, but you should understand your core strengths and find a co-founder to complement them. (Fifteen years ago, I would not have considered myself a good public speaker. I didn't even care for it. Now, I'm good at it and I look forward to it. This only happened because I had to practice and speak in front of people out of necessity, so any skill you want to acquire you can, but over time and with practice.)

Another important aspect to keep in mind when it comes to choosing the right cofounder is geographical proximity. While coworkers can live in a different state or even country, the cofounder needs to be physically close. At this very early stage, you will need to solve one problem after another, and there is nothing more efficient and energizing than collaborating, brainstorming, planning, and solving problems with each other in the same room. As you make progress, there is an energy level that you feed off that cannot be replicated with any virtual collaboration option available. In-person communication and collaboration also aids in solving disputes faster.

Something you have to focus on from the beginning is finances. Either of you being in a bad financial situation can dramatically slow down progress or bring the side venture to a halt. If you have followed my advice in the previous chapters, you have already made sure you are in good financial health at this stage. Now you have to make sure your cofounder is in good financial health as well. Asking them the following questions will help you establish their financial situation: Are they able to commit to this without impacting family and other priorities? How are they supporting themselves and their family? If they are married, would their significant other be OK if they were to commit time and money to this side venture? If things are going extremely well and you are ready to quit your jobs, how long can the both of you go without a salary? Have these hard conversations up front to avoid any potential future disputes that can pose serious threats down the line.

You should have an idea for the type of company and culture you want to create and the value system you want to put in place. Discussing culture and values will help you understand if your potential cofounder has similar values or not. Do you want to focus on the customer or the product? Do you want to create an organization with clear titles and hierarchy or an organization where titles don't matter? Do you want to allow pets in the office? How do you want meetings to be structured? What criteria do you want to use to make hiring decisions? There is a lot to think about here. The goal is to be aligned on the most important terms and conditions, as both of you will have things you like and hate from your current corporate jobs that you either want to keep or can't wait to do differently.

Once you have identified your cofounder and they have agreed to come on board, the first task is to discuss, negotiate, and document the terms. Do not do anything without legal documentation, even if your cofounder is your twin. Start with agreeing on titles and roles. Tiles are fairly insignificant at this stage, as you will both wear many hats, but once you begin talking to customers, investors, and vendors, titles carry certain clout that can help move things forward. Are you the CEO and your cofounder the CTO? Maybe you are the CTO and COO and your cofounder is CEO and CMO? Titles also help loosely define your primary roles and responsibilities, but again, you both need to be ready to take on any task.

Once you have agreed on how roles and responsibilities will be divided, you need to discuss equity. This is extremely important, as how company ownership is divided needs to be fair to prevent any animosity down the line. Both time and money should be the driving factor. You have spent many hours and your own money thus far, which should be factored in. At the same time, you might be lucky and your cofounder is also willing to put up $500,000 to fund the company. This might end up with your cofounder owning controlling interest in the company—meaning more than 50 percent. You need to think about what is best for the company and not for your ego and agree on the percentage split during this initial conversation.

Talk about the big goals and why you are creating this company. Discuss your thoughts at this moment in time regarding sales and marketing strategy and how you will get your product into the market. What is your growth strategy? How will you measure success at various stages? How will you know you have achieved your goals? Do you agree on the target market?

Then, define and agree on your key milestones. You should develop a roadmap with a clear project plan and due dates. In the link at the end of this chapter, I have provided a project plan template that has worked effectively for me. But don't overdo it with a lengthy list that goes out five years. That is unrealistic. At this stage, you can only plan the next three to six months. Your priority will be building the product, testing it, and getting feedback to continue to validate your idea. You will likely have to pivot based on the feedback that is coming in—another reason you should not try to have a lengthy roadmap.

Discussing all of these with your cofounder can be uncomfortable and, in some cases, it might even cause them to leave the project. It is better for this to happen now rather than later when it is too late. After all, being aligned on the goals and vision is vital as you set the foundation of this partnership before going on the entrepreneurial journey together.

Visit the below link for a chapter summary and resources related to this chapter.

www.ch9resources.sideadventure.com

Chapter 10

Building a Prototype

"Unless you have fixed costs, you don't need any capital to create a prototype. Ideally, your cofounders, with sweat equity, can create the product themselves." Brian Chesky

"Your most unhappy customers are your greatest source of learning." Bill Gates

---

After a few years in the corporate world, I started to feel like I was not aligned with my goals and ambitions. I was a couple of years removed from graduating from film school, and what I had visualized while in film school was not the reality I was living. Michael had also entered the corporate world with me and was feeling the same, so we started talking about what to do and we naturally landed on putting more focus on writing scripts.

We put many ideas on the table and then decided which one was worth pursuing. We spent hours at Starbucks and other locations building up the characters and their character arc, the storylines, and everything else that goes into writing a movie script. After a couple of years, we had two very solid scripts. Now what? We thought of how we would go about shopping our scripts, and it was difficult. We quickly found that it's not what you know, it's *who* you know. We persisted, and eventually we received a couple of opportunities. The first script we had finished was a horror movie, and we found a producer who was looking for a horror film project. After the initial meeting, things looked bright as the producer asked for a minor rewrite but after the second and third meetings, they ended up passing. Looking back, it made sense why they passed. This was around the mid-2000s and the industry was shifting toward streaming with the launch of Netflix and YouTube gaining popularity, so big studios making small horror films by first-time writers was not a good business decision—this was also around the same time Disney bought Pixar and Marvel to back up the strategy of producing big blockbuster franchise films.

The second script we had written was an animated script, so naturally we started with the biggest animation studio. Prior to buying Pixar, Disney was going through a rough patch with their animation movies and their relationship with Pixar. We successfully met with animated film producers who loved our idea and asked us to come back with sequel ideas, which were also very well received at a second meeting. The producers told us that their research department had to go through a due diligence process to see what was happening in the industry before moving forward. To us, that was a great sign, and we left the meeting excited. We nervously waited for roughly two weeks. Finally, we heard back and we were told that the research department had discovered that another studio was already in production of an animated feature with a similar concept and they were not going to move forward with us. We were extremely bummed—it turned out that the movie was *Madagascar*, which made us even more upset since our story was very different, with animals from a zoo as the only commonality.

The lesson we learned from these two experiences was how important it is to be aware of market conditions, industry shifts, and the business world in general. It didn't take long for me to realize that Web 2.0 was going to change the internet and enable many new products and services. From an investor's perspective, that is where more money was being pushed, so I started to educate myself about software entrepreneurship. I found many common elements between being a filmmaker and being an entrepreneur. Essentially, filmmakers are entrepreneurs, and the product they are building is content.

All I did, 24 hours a day, even in my dreams, was come up with ideas. I would wake up from a dream and write down the idea I had. I then started flushing out a few of the ideas only using PowerPoint slides, trying to convince friends and acquaintances to invest. I got a lot of "that's a great idea" but not a single dollar. I could not figure out why. If they thought the ideas were so good, why were they not supporting me? It was because they did not know if I could execute the idea. I'm not a designer and I'm not a developer, so there was no reason for friends to have confidence that my idea would turn into a real product. They were thinking with their investor hat on, which had nothing to do with not being my friends.

My competitive side kicked in and I wanted to prove them wrong. Without trying or even understanding how to validate the idea, I started using my own money to develop websites and products. The initial attempt was a hot mess and I was glad I had not taken any money from friends and family. The next three attempts were also failures, mainly because I was not validating my ideas. I had learned how to build a prototype to not only be able to talk about the idea in a tangible way but to demonstrate my ability to execute it. With no track record, you will need a prototype. It was a great working prototype that eventually led to $4 million in total investments in my hospitality software company.

What exactly is a prototype? In software development, a prototype is a working model of your product. It is the intersection between your idea and the MVP. Experienced engineers and startup founders will probably build a prototype that has a database and backend. In your case, your prototype will just be the interactive frontend User Interface (UI) that gives the illusion there is a database and a backend. This is the most low-cost approach to building a prototype. The primary goal of your prototype is to help you flesh out the key features before building the MVP and to demonstrate that you are capable of execution.

There are some key questions that you need to answer before jumping into your prototype. These will help you refine your idea and force you to think about how to deliver a unique value proposition.

- How do you see your product solving the problem?
- What is the business model and how will you generate revenue?
- What are the main features and how will they work together?
- What are the various pages of the software?
- Who will you get feedback from as you build the prototype and what is your feedback loop?
- Who are potential customers and users you will demonstrate the final prototype to? Getting potential customers and users involved in the prototype process will be the most valuable information and feedback you receive.
- What metrics will help you decide you are on the right track?
- Who can help you raise capital to build the MVP if you cannot self-fund?

You might be extremely excited about your idea and want to build the actual product as soon as you can, but there are many benefits to a prototype, especially for first-time entrepreneurs.

The prototype allows you to fine-tune your design and functionality. In most cases, what you have in your head doesn't work in reality. You'll never know the issues and challenges until you actually take your idea from theory to reality.

You gain clarity and focus while building a prototype. You begin to understand what information and content is needed on each page. You also become clear on the types of users you need to support—for example, there might be different features for an admin compared to a regular user.

You will also improve on how to effectively describe your product. Your main home page will be a marketing and sales landing page. It needs to have various marketing copy. Iterate and get as much feedback as you can on your copy, as it is the first impression your product makes.

When you present anyone a prototype, they will undoubtedly take you more seriously. It shows that you are dedicated and able to execute. It will also separate you from the majority who talk about ideas but have nothing to show for them.

On top of being a way to validate the execution of your idea, a prototype also acts as the planning process of your eventual MVP. Handing over a prototype to a designer and a developer will guarantee a smoother development process and minimize miscommunication and direction getting lost in translation, which equates to speed and cost. It also allows a developer to provide feedback on what is possible and what is not.

To build the actual prototype, you do not need to be a designer or developer. You just need to be determined, have the right tools, and know the steps.

Step 1 is research. You have to study and become obsessed with competitor products. Sign up and use them so you have an intimate understanding of their inner workings. Gather information about the features, business models, what actual customers are saying, and which features they started with. Get inspiration on how you would design your prototype.

Step 2 is making a list of the features that you think are needed in your prototype. As you begin building the prototype, be cautious of scope creep. Scope creep is when you add features to a product that increase the time to build and test but are not necessary to drive your value proposition. This is an area where most first-time entrepreneurs stumble. You only need features that deliver on your value proposition and solve the problem you are intending to solve. If you are not able to do this with your core features, adding more features will not get you there.

Step 3 is to identify user groups. You can differentiate them by age, need, frequency, and information. For example, a social media marketing manager is using Facebook and Instagram differently compared to your mom or aunt, and your mom or aunt is using Instagram differently compared to teens. Understanding these different user personas will help you make important design and feature decisions now that will eventually save you money and time when you are ready to hire a vendor to build your MVP.

Step 4 is to create sketches of the main pages of your web or mobile app. By this point, you should be intimately familiar with competitors or similar products and have a list of pages and features you believe are needed in your prototype. Now it's time to put them on paper. There are tools to do this digitally, but I have found that a pencil and paper still work the best—the intention is not aesthetics. You want to get a rough idea of what buttons and call to actions you need on each page. What are the navigation links that are needed? Will there be static or dynamic content? How many sections are needed? Your mind should be going at 100 MPH as you begin to truly visualize your product. As you think of something, it will trigger a thought you had not had before and since you are using a pencil you can quickly erase and iterate your thoughts on the fly. Again, don't try to fully flush out the entire page on this step. You just want a rough sketch to help you in the next step. If you have a potential user or a trusted and experienced individual by your side, this would be a good opportunity to get some feedback, as they will help you think about dependencies you might not have thought about.

Step 5 is to turn your sketch into a wireframe and create flow charts for important features to capture the user's journey. A wireframe is the skeleton of your UI. I usually use a tool to create a wireframe. There is a link at the end of this chapter with a list of tools you can choose from that I find work well for me. The reason I use a tool to create wireframes is because most tools have helpful tips that act as a coach. A digital wireframe also allows you to connect pages so you can visually see what happens when a button is clicked and how different pages interact. A wireframe also helps you better understand the dependencies an action has and what potential business rules you might want to apply.

I'm going to use a simple social media example to explain this point. There is a very active user on a popular social media platform that has been uploading content and engaging with other users for months. One day, they click a button to delete or deactivate their account. What happens with all the content they uploaded? What happens with all the comments they have left? These are the types of dependencies you have to think through. If a feature is complex, the best thing to do is to think in an operational mindset. Create a flowchart that shows you step by step the user's journey and all dependencies of a feature. This will help you figure out what elements are needed on the various pages to support the feature. In general, you should map out the journey of the various user types in the different parts of your product. If you require a user to register, what are the steps they need to go through? Thinking in a workflow mindset will help you see right away the number of steps you are asking a user to take, thus allowing you to make sure the process is as simple and intuitive as possible.

You are finally at step 6 and ready to create your prototype. If this sounds like you have to do a lot of work to just get the prototype together, it's because it is indeed a lot of work. At each step, you get the opportunity to fine-tune your product, get feedback, and further validate your problem statement and your value proposition at a very low cost. Because you have done all the leg work in the prototyping process, translating your vision to a designer will be easier. Before you pass on your wireframe to a designer, you need to make some decisions. I will go deeper into branding in a later chapter, but you do need to make some early branding decisions at this stage. You can always change them as you get feedback, but these decisions will help the designer.

There are a few options when trying to convert your wireframes into a User Interface/User Experience (UI/UX) prototype. This means there is no database and no servers and computing power. Option one is to use a prototyping tool—the link at the end of this chapter offers you a list. What is great about these tools is that you can make changes quickly, and some of them offer design templates to choose from—but they can be time-consuming, and since you want the prototype to be great and not just good enough, templates are probably not the best route to go.

Option two is to hire someone to create the prototype for you—we will go into more details in the next chapter about selecting and hiring vendors, as you will have to do this at some point. The advantage with this option is that, assuming you have gone through a selection process to choose the right vendor, it's less of a time commitment and you gain expertise, but there is a cost involved and you will have to manage the vendor.

The third option is what I prefer, which is a hybrid of options one and two. I look for a vendor or freelancer that is both a designer and an expert in the prototyping tool I use most often. This option will not only cost less than option two, but I also have a professional designer working with me and I can go into the tool and have transparency on progress at all times. I can also contribute and make changes myself—and not be fully dependent on someone who is most likely in a different time zone to make all the changes I want.

The value a prototype with functioning design provides is another low-cost way to get feedback and validate your problem statement. Get your prototype in front of as many friends, family members, and potential customers and users as you can. The magic number for me is about 100 people. As you meet with each person, make sure you are documenting the feedback so you can then analyze it holistically—I use Excel to capture notes and feedback. The template I use can be found in the link at the end of this chapter. The questions below will help you find crucial answers.

- Did your test group agree with the problem statement? This should be a yes based on your previous steps, but it's good to validate every chance you get.

- Did your test group believe your product solves the problem? If you do not have an overwhelming majority say yes, you need to go back to the drawing board.

- Did your test group like the design and branding? Design is important to people. Most people can't explain or quantify why they like or don't like a design—but they know if they do or don't. This is your first opportunity to test your design and branding and receive feedback.

- Did your test group think your product was too complex or had too many features? Customers and users describing a product as too complex is a clear sign that either your design is not intuitive or you have jammed too many features into the prototype. Fancy bells and whistles might sound interesting, but when it comes down to it, they are not necessary and do more damage than good.

- What are the only features your test group said they need? This will help you get to a product that is simple and more intuitive in the eyes of your users and customers.

- Does your prototype do one thing and do it extremely well or are you trying to do many things at the same time? Don't get caught up in the excitement of future versions or comparing yourself to established products and brands that are now solving many problems. Your product only has to do one thing and do it well.

- If your business model is to charge for your product, would your test group pay for it? And if so, how much? This is a great opportunity to capture data to inform your pricing strategy, revenue model, and forecast for your investor pitch deck.

- What did you learn about your product, your demographics, and your market? If you pay close attention to the feedback you always learn something that you didn't know or think about before.

- How should you modify your prototype before proceeding to build your MVP?

If the feedback you received was not what you hoped for, then you need to take a hard look at what the issue is and make a decision at this step to go back to the drawing board to revamp your prototype and go through another round of testing, pivot to a modified version of your prototype, or abandon the idea before spending more money and time on it. By being laser-focused on the problem and the market, you increase the chances of a successful MVP and a cheaper development process.

Visit the below link for a chapter summary and resources related to this chapter.

www.ch10resources.sideadventure.com

CHAPTER 11

FINDING A VENDOR

"Master your strengths, outsource your
weaknesses." Ryan Khan

"The other part of outsourcing is this: it
simply says where the work can be done
outside better than it can be done inside, we
should do it." Alphonso Jackson

When I decided to make a change and pursue building a software product instead of filmmaking, I had very little experience in finding, qualifying, and selecting a vendor. Not having a background in design and coding, I knew I needed help from experts in these fields.

Having only an idea and not having done the due diligence I have described in the previous chapters, I jumped on Google and, after hours of searching and reading, I stumbled on an individual that claimed to have an existing code he was selling for very low cost, which he would then help customize at a low cost. Being as naive as I was over fifteen years ago, I thought this was great. It was like taking an Excel template and modifying it to avoid having to start from scratch. Boy was I wrong. I wasted a year going down this route—I will help you avoid these missteps with what I'm going to share with you in this chapter.

If you are building a blog or an e-commerce site, many off-the-shelf tools and templates can help you get started fast, like Shopify, Wix, and Square, but building a custom product with existing code from someone in another country is definitely not a good idea. The person I bought the code from claimed they were from Australia, which I thought was great since language would not be a problem, but I did not validate this and it turned out he did not live in Australia. The signs that my project was going to fail were there from day one, but being inexperienced I did not see them and was taken for a ride. He hosted the code on his own server—or so he claimed—and since I did not know much about hosting and servers at the time, I took his word for it.

At first, he was responsive and I could see changes I was requesting were being made—albeit poorly—and then I had to chase and chase to get it to an OK place. It was like pulling teeth. After months of chasing, bad communication, not having access to the server, and a product that was nothing like I had envisioned, I cut my losses and dropped the project. But I learned some valuable lessons.

Meanwhile, at my corporate job, I started managing vendors to perform media services and saw first-hand how a good vendor can become your partner and the role I had to play to make sure we were successful. Whether I was buying media services or software services, the principles of selecting and managing vendors were the same. Shortly after this awful experience, I got promoted and was given the responsibility of evaluating and selecting vendors through a process called Request for Proposal (RFP). This is a process in which you outline in great detail what services you need and your expectations and ask vendors to submit a proposal against your RFP. You then need to have a way to score and measure the responses you receive from the various vendors and suppliers participating in the RFP.

For a large media company, this can be a lengthy process, but I knew this was exactly what I needed to do for my next idea—although I had to simplify it for a quick response. I had also been exposed to software development and how they went from a concept to prototype to validation before building a robust product. In addition, I was doing a lot of reading and taking online courses so I knew that, for my next attempt, I had to start out with a prototype—but I still had not failed enough times to understand the whole process.

For my next idea, I posted a job on a freelance community website inviting vendors to bid on building a very small part of my prototype I had sketched on paper and mocked up in Excel. Within a few hours, I got over fifty proposals that, from a price and timing perspective, had a wide range. My first step was to eliminate proposals from accounts that had no feedback. From the balance of the proposals, almost all vendors and freelancers had a five-star rating, which told me the rating and feedback system could be used as a way to qualify a vendor, but it can not be the only way. I then looked at the accounts that had the most projects completed, as that was a better indication that their star rating was mostly organic instead of manufactured.

I decided to award the project to five different proposals. The prices ranged from $30 to $100, so in total I probably spent $300. My goal with this approach was to test out a vendor on a small scale before wasting a lot more money and time on the larger project. It also allowed me to vet out individuals versus firms. Once you go through this process, you will see that the lower-priced proposals are either from individuals that are thinking short-term and not operating a business or from individuals and firms that are just trying to get the project. They know the project scope will likely change once you get into it and they can bill you more because it is unlikely you are going to scrap the project at this stage. I also provided them with a simple RFP as part of my evolution effort.

It was obvious from the beginning who I did not want to work with because the communication was not on par with my expectations. After a week, I was down to two firms. I ended up asking both to build another part of the prototype so I could get more data to evaluate their performance. Within two weeks, I had my selection—I continue to work with this firm to date. Since then, I've done similar exercises with firms and vendors in other countries known for strong design and engineering talent and have built a network that I leverage. As a result, I know first-hand the general pros and cons of outsourcing to several countries. If you are in a similar place where I was over fifteen years ago, your only option is to outsource as well—but let's talk about what your options are.

The first and more widely known option is offshore development, also known as outsourcing. This is where you hire a third party—an individual or a company—to perform services for you. For this book, we are specifically talking about design and software development services. Outsourcing doesn't necessarily mean the third party is in another country—you can outsource your bookkeeping to an accountant that lives in the same city—but offshore development is specific to hiring a third party in another country. If the project you have outsourced is small, you will probably have a couple of people that are working on your project part-time, as they are assigned multiple projects. If your project is large, you can request a dedicated team.

The second commonly known option is the IT staffing model, meaning if you bring someone on-board to be part of the team—full-time or part-time—for a temp period or without an end date, working remotely on some aspect of developing the product. This process should be no different than hiring an employee—which has its own challenges.

As the project evolves and grows, you will probably end up with a hybrid model of outsourcing, IT staffing, and having a distributed team, but at a very early stage when you are just trying to build a prototype and MVP, hiring a single vendor and outsourcing all aspects of development is your best option. In some cases, the vendor might have employees that have a high level of technical knowledge and experience but not a good eye for design. You will then need to go through the same evaluation process to find someone or a firm to outsource the UI design to. Unlike development, where I do not recommend working with an individual, finding an individual to do the initial design for you can work. As with any decision or option, there are pros and cons of outsourcing your prototype and MVP to an offshore development vendor as well. Let's start with the pros.

Cost savings. When you outsource your development to an offshore team, you instantly reap the benefits of lower cost of living compared to the United States. For example, in the United States, an agency will charge well above $100 per hour compared to $10–30 per hour for offshore development. In addition, you will not have the typical overhead of office rent, equipment, insurance, and all other costs associated with hiring employees. Every dollar is going toward building your prototype and MVP, which is where you need to be spending your limited funds.

Increase capacity. As you begin the development process, each week you might need different resources. With outsourcing, the vendor is responsible for all the day-to-day operational duties and making sure they can add resources to the project when needed, leaving you free to focus only on the prototype and MVP.

Time to market. Getting your prototype and MVP out to market fast is critical. You have to approach your venture with urgency because there is competition, even if you are not aware of it yet. Instead of having to spend weeks and months building a team, outsourcing allows you to jump right in and focus on the product. When you outsource to an offshore team, the time zone difference can also become an advantage and speed up the process if set up the right way. For me, India gave me this advantage.

Reliability. Of course, this depends on the firm and how well you evaluated them, but you can count on the good firms and vendors to have an experienced team ready to work on your product as soon as you form an agreement with them. If there is illness or turnover within their teams, which will happen, they have established processes to cover for a person out sick or fill an open role with little impact on your project. This allows you to focus on the product instead of other internal operational needs.

Now let's touch on some of the challenges you will face.

Communication. Because of language barriers, even if your main point of contact has strong English skills, it is easy for your directions, requirements, and requests to get lost in translation, leading to both time and money lost if not managed properly, and the proper risk mitigation steps implemented. Because of time zone differences, communication also may not happen as frequently as it should, leading to an issue taking longer to resolve.

Technology gaps. Having your product developed on older hardware and software can cause significant issues when you are ready to launch your product into the market. Due to budgets, offshore teams might not have the latest software and hardware.

Quality. This topic is always controversial when discussed in the context of offshore development. What you need to remember is that quality is less about the country and more about the team and how involved and diligent you are in the testing process. If you are expecting an offshore team to do R&D (Research and Development) for you and innovate with your budget, you will be disappointed. Offshore teams are great at building your prototype and MVP so you can test your idea quickly and with a low budget. Beyond the MVP stage, the offshore team can continue to play a critical role, but you will need on-shore engineers and developers. If you are able to get past the MVP stage, your product will become more complex. This is where the risk of low quality with an offshore vendor will have an impact on the speed of development, which you might not be able to afford.

Management. You have to be very hands-on to make sure your project is moving forward. This can be difficult when your project is starting as a side venture, but the lack of daily oversight and management will lead to failure. Great communication, tools, processes, and metrics need to be established and enforced to drastically improve the chances of success.

Testing. This is where I felt the most frustration, and it will probably be the same for you. If you are testing an app and something doesn't work correctly, with an in-house developer you can just go see them in person, show your experience, and the developer will most likely implement a fix very quickly. With offshore development, conveying a bug is not as simple. You can create a ticket, but they are not able to reproduce it on your end. You end up going back and forth with screenshots and videos to finally troubleshoot and resolve. The iPhone now has a feature where you can record the actions you perform—I wish I had this feature years ago. Use this feature and video your desktop monitors every time you report a bug to reduce the back and forth. Most importantly, you must remain patient and do the work during testing to provide as much information as possible so the bug can be fixed with minimal back and forth.

Security. With data protection being so critical, it is harder to maintain data security with offshore vendors. Once you are beyond the MVP stage, the very least you have to do is hire an auditor to audit the code, data model, and security to help you establish a process to be as secure as possible with what your budget allows and compliant with your local laws.

Culture. Not being able to understand the culture of the country your offshore vendor resides in can cause issues for all of the above. If you are from the United States, you are in a low-context culture—meaning that deadlines are very important, decision-making is logical, and change is OK. In contrast, India and China are considered to have high-context cultures, which means that deadlines are less important, decisions are more intuitive, and there can be a resistance to change. Inability to understand and recognize these differences and finding ways to mitigate its impact can lead to frustration and potential abandonment of your project.

Legal. You have less protection with offshore vendors than you do with vendors that reside in your own country. This is because our laws and regulations might not apply to them, so it is important to have all agreements documented and have risk mitigation and contingency plans if a relationship goes sour.

In more than fifteen years working with offshore teams, I've had the opportunity to work with people in many different countries. I have established a friendship with some where I'm asked to visit their hometown so they can show me around and some that I do not have contact with anymore. Overall, even though the failed ventures outweigh the successes, the experience and learnings have all been worth it. The journey is more important than the final destination.

As I have already stated, it's less about the country than the people and your ability to qualify and validate a vendor through a thoughtful RFP process. Of course, your budget will either limit your choice or give you more options. In addition, how simple or complex a product you are trying to build comes into play, as there are fewer senior-level, expensive developers available compared to junior-level, inexpensive developers.

When the topic of outsourcing and offshore development comes up, the regions that get the most attention are Asia and Eastern Europe. In Asia, you will see hourly charges that range from $10–35 compared to the $20–50 per hour rate in Eastern Europe.

Asia. When discussing outsourcing with an outsourcing expert, India is the most talked-about option. India popularized the notion of outsourcing in the 1990s, and about 80 percent of all outsourcing to this region is still going to India. With thousands of computer science graduates every year, there are many skilled people in the industry. They also speak English, but with a local accent and vernacular. Culturally, they are very hard-working, and working long hours is the norm.

Based on my experience, whatever requirements you provide is what you get. It is not part of the culture to regularly question the customer, where in the United States it is accepted and thought of as higher-level critical thinking to take a request and make it better. As a result, the feature you envisioned in your mind and on paper is implemented exactly as such, but now that it is real you may realize it doesn't make sense and you have wasted time and money. This can be managed if you set expectations with the team leads working on your product.

Because of the large pool of engineers, there is high turnover. For one project, I ended up hiring a business analyst, as the project was at a critical stage and they had an offer from another firm with more pay and I was not willing to take the risk to lose that person. There is also the tendency to try to deliver code as quickly as possible to please the client, which sometimes comes with sacrificing quality and testing taking longer. You can mitigate all of these with best practices around communication, management, and expectation setting.

Eastern Europe. Eastern European countries have more recently garnered notoriety in their pool of talented engineers. Their communication style and culture are closer to the style of the United States, thus leading to fewer communication challenges. Countries like Armenia, which geographically is part of western Asia but culturally more like Eastern Europe, are fast becoming tech and innovation hubs.

In general, the talent level is higher in Eastern Europe and culturally OK to question client requests. Depending on your working hours, Eastern Europe time zones can be more difficult to work around compared to Southeast Asia, where a 12-hour difference does make planning calls and requesting responses to emails easier if you live in the West Coast. For example, if you are in California, your 7:30 p.m. is 7:30 a.m. in India, so you can easily have a couple of hours of live communication with your business analysis and project lead compared to 7:30 p.m. in California being 4:30 a.m. in Poland. If you're in New York, Poland is only a 6-hour difference, so it's much easier to work with a vendor in that region. In addition, hourly rates in Eastern Europe are higher than in Southeast Asia, so your budget might not allow you to explore options in Eastern Europe.

Latin America. I have not had much experience with Latin America, as the region is not the primary go-to when you think of offshore development—especially a decade ago—but countries like Mexico, Argentina, and Chile have become popular choices over the last few years. There are time zone advantages if you are in the United States, language is less of a barrier, and it is common for the engineers to have studied in the United States, so they are familiar with United States best practices. But on average, it is the more expensive option.

It is critical that you take the time to make the right vendor selection. I mentioned the RFP process, but there are other best practices you can leverage as part of the RFP process or in parallel with RFP.

When using a platform to hire a firm, make sure you ask your candidates specific questions about the project you have asked them to bid on. Many firms and individual developers will blindly bid on your project without reading your requirements—stay away from these firms and individuals.

Understand that the only difference between hiring someone into the company and hiring an offshore firm is that you need to have an appreciation for the culture of the offshore firm. This is why, if you can, you should visit the offshore team and spend some time with them to get to know the management and the development team. If this is not an option, schedule various video conference calls. As part of these in-person or video conference conversations, you need to have clear goals and objectives as to what you want to get out of them.

Read every customer review on the platform you are using. Also, select two or three customers that have left a review and request private feedback. It is common that the reviews might be manufactured or inflated, so a private request can give you more information that is closer to the reality than the public review to help with your selection process.

In addition to their customer reviews, study the work samples available on the platform. Also, request more samples that might not be available publicly. Since I only work with firms, I also do a Google search to see what information I can find on the company, including social media pages and any information I can dig up to help me with my decision-making.

Make sure they have a clear understanding of current technologies and best practices. If you have no way of making a judgment and neither does your cofounder, ask a friend or colleague with more technical acumen to join you on a call with the firm. A few questions from an experienced person will quickly reveal if the people at the firm keep up with technology and trends or not.

Whether you meet them in person or on your video conference calls, get a clear understanding of the key individuals and the structure of the firm. Ask who would be working on your project and have a five-minute conversation with these individuals. If you are not given access to anyone besides the owner, GM, or someone that is trying to get the contract and close a sale, consider it a red flag.

Ask the firm about their workflow and procedures, and check if they keep any performance metrics, have any Service Level Agreements (SLAs), how they manage scaling up or down, and about tools they use to manage communication and projects. These questions are intended to give you an idea of how sophisticated and mature their operation is. The communication and project management capabilities of the vendor you choose will make or break your project.

If you are someone who is in a similar position as I was, getting started with your venture in the offshore development operating model is the best solution. But don't fall in love with this model. As you gain traction with your product and have either raised funding or are generating revenue that allows you to hire team members, you need to start balancing the offshore development team with in-house developers. You will gain speed and quality with in-house developers, which does come at a price, but with a product that has traction, you need to pay that price to scale and grow quickly to capture or penetrate your desired market before your competition does.

Visit the below link for a chapter summary and resources related to this chapter.

www.ch11resources.sideadventure.com

CHAPTER 12

DEVELOPMENT AND TESTING

"Walking on water and developing software
from a specification are easy if both are
frozen." Edward V Berard

"Design is not just what it looks like and feels
like. Design is how it works." Steve Jobs

Y ou have done your due diligence and have signed an agreement with an offshore development firm. By now you should have good documentation on what you want to build, so just pass these documents to them and wait for the magic to happen, right? Not really. Things only get harder and more complicated as you progress. Managing an offshore development team is, in essence, a specialized version of vendor management. If, as part of your job, you are responsible for managing vendors, you already have the basics down. If you have not had any experience in managing vendors, I recommend diving deeper into it with the reading material I have provided at the end of this chapter, as the success of your product and company at this point is almost 100 percent dependent on your ability to manage an offshore development team.

I was lucky that, as part of my corporate job, managing large vendors and supply chains was a primary responsibility. Having done this for over fifteen years, I do consider myself an expert and have even spoken about this topic at various events. I also had the opportunity to develop internal systems at my corporate job, which gave me a good understanding and experience for how to couple these two skills and experiences into successfully managing an offshore development team. Before I get into some core best practices, I want to help you understand how most offshore development teams are structured.

Your primary contact will be the project manager (PM). This person will make sure your project is going as planned and help resolve issues if they are not. They will be the person to take your communication and feedback and relay it to the appropriate person, help coordinate calls, create agendas, and help address risks. You will most likely develop a close relationship with this person if they have reliable PM skills.

Depending on the size of your MVP, you might have a business analyst, or the PM and the business analyst might be the same person. The term Product Owner is often used as well. Their responsibility is to make sure they understand your goals and vision and your requirements and translate them to the developers. They will also manage the backlog of items that need to be developed or fixed and all the issues that might arise during your testing process. A good business analyst or product owner will take your requirements and improve on them.

At a high level, development teams are separated between back-end and front-end, with each having its own team lead. As the name suggests, the front-end development team is responsible for the overall visual look and feel of the software— commonly known as UI and UX. The team lead is responsible for managing all the developers in this team and maintaining regular communication with the PM, the Business Analyst, and the team lead for the back-end developers, who are responsible for everything that is under the hood. This includes the code that makes the software interactive, the APIs, and all aspects of the database and the server. The team lead manages the developers and ensures correct integration with the UI/UX and works closely with the PM, Business Analyst, and the front-end team lead.

A critical person or team for the development is DevOps. This person or team is essentially responsible for setting up and maintaining the server, creating and managing the operational workflows for the developers to work in, making sure the server has adequate security measures, dealing with system crashes, and ensuring that the software is built in a way that can scale with more users.

The final core team is the Quality Assurance (QA) team. This team is responsible for making sure your requirements were translated correctly and checking the functionality and that UI/UX work as intended before they release the new code for you to test. They are also responsible for responding to issues you may find in your testing.

When it comes to the actual process of development, there are a few methodologies. The most common are waterfall development and agile development. I have provided suggested reading at the end of this chapter if you are interested in diving deep into these, but in short, waterfall development is where each step in the process is performed sequentially and you don't move forward until you are done with the step you are in. For example, you must document all requirements first before design can start. On the other hand, agile development, as the name suggests, is more agile. Its goal is to develop in small chunks—called sprints—through the collaboration of the various teams, taking into account that the product will evolve as you begin seeing parts of it in action.

My preference is the agile methodology, and I highly suggest that you hire a firm that practices it in their operations. There is little chance that how you initially envisioned your product actually ends up being the MVP that finds product market fit. This is because there are so many dependencies that it is hard to visualize everything up front. It is to your advantage to develop in sprints to allow you the opportunity to iterate and improve on the fly. This also makes testing easier, as you are focused on testing specific functionality. It will also be less costly, as there will be a lower number of change requests. Waiting to test once most of the product is built not only will slow down your release, but will end up costing more. To be successful in the agile methodology, planning becomes crucial, so you will work with the PM and the Business Analyst to plan two to three weeks of activity in advance.

Taking these steps will improve your chances of success in working with the offshore development team you have hired. My biggest takeaway after all these years is that you should never assume the PM or Business Analyst understands your instructions. You need to be proactive and take additional steps and ask the right questions to ensure you are being understood correctly—communicate as much as possible, but simplify the communication. Don't forget that no matter how fluent their English might appear, they are still part of a different culture. There is a language barrier, so try to understand their use of vocabulary and adapt to it. Simplify the words you are using and be direct and clear with your directions and requests. Be as specific as possible with your user stories and specs and use visuals all the time. Do not rely on just words to get your point across. I'll provide you with some examples at the end of this chapter.

Given the importance of communication, you must find a way to overlap your schedule with their schedule and ensure you can have real-time communication during part of their workday. This is all based on your schedule and the time difference between you and your offshore development firm. If you are smart about how you leverage the time difference, it can become a real advantage. To give you an example, someone from the western United States has hired an Indian firm. Given the month, this person is between twelve-and-a-half to thirteen-and-a-half hours behind India, as India does not observe daylight savings. With a nine-to-six corporate job schedule, this person can ask their offshore team to work an 8:30 a.m. to 6 p.m. schedule, which means they can have four or more hours—depending on how late they sleep—overlap with the India team office hours.

Delays are inevitable in software development, especially when it is an early-stage startup, so instead of trying to avoid delays, it is better to try to manage the risk associated with the delays by setting clear goals and deadlines, using metrics to manage performance, and being aware of the bigger picture. Let's say you have a product demo scheduled in six weeks. You might have an internal deadline for when you want to be ready for this demo. This shouldn't be the same deadline for the development team. Their deadline should be a few days before. This way, you are mitigating the risk that development delay will impact your scheduled demo.

You need to use a set of tools to manage the various processes and communication. Relying on email, Excel, and Word alone will not cut it. Before work starts, you need to discuss and agree on the following: How will you conduct phone and video conferencing calls? Popular options are Skype, Zoom, Slack, and Bluejeans—but there are others. Some might have a small monthly fee while some have free options. Determine which one will work best for you—my priorities were ease of use, easy screen sharing, and the ability to record meetings for future reference.

At the same level of importance, within the communication toolset, is what you use for chatting. My preference is Slack, as it has become the industry standard, but there are other options.

I found the way you can organize different communication threads and search within older conversations for keywords and documents was very helpful and saved me a lot of time. You will not be able to avoid the use of emails, but set boundaries for what email should be used for. Avoid lengthy emails, as it is easy for points to be missed or misunderstood. Do not use emails to report bugs, issues, or new requests.

What I have used for managing user stories, sprints, and bugs is Jira—the project management tool. I found this tool to work best for my working style, but I wouldn't call Jira the most intuitive. If your product is simple, you might want to go with Trello but again, test out a few and see what works for you and your offshore development firm. If you are quick to learn new tools, something you might want to consider is adapting to what your offshore team is already using, as on-boarding and training a team to use a new tool has its own challenges.

No matter what you end up deciding on, you must establish business rules around the usage of your toolset. For example, in Jira, there are various ways you can create a priority list. Also, certain terminology might have different meanings, so you need to be aligned. For example, if a feature has been moved to the category "In testing," what does this mean? Is it ready for you to test or is it in internal testing? Establishing these business rules is important, but know that it cannot all happen overnight, especially if you are new to the tools. As the project evolves, you can establish new business rules, but make sure there is a method to clearly communicate them and get agreement from your offshore development team.

You want to have access to the latest code at all times. Not only is this a way to mitigate the risk if things go sour with the vendor you have chosen, but it will also allow you to audit the code when the time comes. You can store your code in the cloud, GitHub, or other platforms. You will determine this as part of the DevOps process and when the end-to-end development workflow is being established at the onset of the project. What is important is that you are the admin of whatever platform you end up going with.

You need to be extra proactive to set the tone. Given the time difference, the offshore team can never be in a situation where they are waiting for days for your response or direction. You have to be one step ahead and anticipate what they might need to turn the time difference into a strength instead of a weakness.

You need to be disciplined to stick to the MVP. This will ensure the offshore team has a higher chance of hitting your deadlines. With every sprint, you will get new ideas, but remember you can't just squeeze in every idea—unless you remove something else. Communicate your vision to the offshore team so they can help make your vision even better and stay on track. This will only happen if you open the door and welcome ideas and suggestions, as that might not be the culture they are used to.

You and your team need to have the same environment that your offshore team is using for development and testing. If you are testing an iPhone app on an iPhone X that has the latest iOS while they are testing on an iPhone 8 and not the latest iOS, this can lead to a he-said-she-said situation, as you are seeing issues your offshore team is not, which leads to a lot of time wasted. Make sure everything is consistent.

Last but not least, use agile methodology. For example, if you have followed my advice, on top of your prototype as reference, you should also have detailed and thorough documentation, user stories, and wireframes, which you have received initial feedback on from potential customers and users. These are what you will be using to communicate your intent with the PM and Business Analyst so they can provide you with a cost estimate.

Once you have worked out the cost and agreed to it, you are ready to begin development.

The first decision you need to make is where your product will be hosted. The trend and best practice right now are to go with cloud hosting. When Amazon's AWS created this industry, they were the only option, so I prefer AWS, but there are other options today—Google Cloud and Microsoft Azure. You should combine your own research with what your offshore development team has experience in to make this decision.

Once you have created your account, you can give the offshore team access to it, but make sure you always have account ownership. There are tools that can help you estimate your monthly cloud expenses to help with your budgeting. The DevOp's person or team will have to create two identical environments—one is the QA environment and the other the production environment. QA environment is for in-progress work and testing while production is the version of the product that will be consumer-facing. As part of the DevOps process, you need to think about security and development workflows. Don't try to act like a large corporation and create a highly secure environment—it will be a waste of time and money. You want to be aware of the type of security you will eventually need so the developers can build your product with that future in mind.

There are privacy and data security laws in every country, so understand what the requirements are in your country and make sure the offshore development team is aware of them as well. As far as the development workflow, you want to make sure the proper version control process is set up as well as a tight process for code to be archived. Request a workflow diagram to be drawn so you can see the workflow visually. Adjust the workflow as needed if you see that it is not as efficient as it should be.

At the same time, the programming language that will be used needs to be determined. If you are like me during my first side venture, all programming language was a foreign language to me. I did not know the difference, so use both your offshore development team and your own independent research to get a high-level understanding of what programming language is common at the time. You can also reference a competitor to see what they are using to guide you to a decision. If your product is only a mobile app, the decision is easy, as Apple and Google have already established what programming language needs to be used to build an app on their platform.

If your product will have a mobile app, you should not begin by building an iOS and Android app at the same time. You should start with just one platform, and once you have product market fit, you can work on scaling. Things to consider are ease of testing and which platform has a larger market share for your demographic in your country or region. Your product will evolve, and you will have pivots until you have product market fit. Having to go through this process with multiple mobile apps will be both time consuming and a waste of your budget. Having said that, there are tools and services like React Native that allow you to build once and deploy on multiple platforms, but this is a more specialized skill that will probably impact your cost as well.

You must establish the expectation that everything being built needs to be documented. Think of it as having an architectural blueprint for a building. You might decide to change your vendor or are in a position to hire internal engineers or want a third party to audit your code. These documents are critical to ensuring how the product has been built and to quickly find and access specific code.

Once your development environments are established, you understand the development workflow, and there is agreement on the programming language or mobile strategy, you will work with the PM and Business Analyst to create a product roadmap. This is a high-level view of which pieces will be built during each sprint that establishes how many sprints it will take to build the MVP, thus ending up with a completion ETA. As development is fluid, the ETA will not be an actual date but an estimate of how many weeks or months the project will take. This roadmap is also the scope of work, which can be added to your contract as a Statement of Work (SOW).

Now that you have a high-level breakdown and roadmap for the project, you can move to your first sprint planning. This should be in a software project management tool. Every feature and component being built during that sprint will be added as an item to the tool you are using with very detailed user stories, wireframes, and any other visuals possible to reduce the chance of anything being lost in translation. The PM has more work to do during this planning step, as they need to ensure the right resources are available, contingency plans are in place in case a resource is out, and any other task that is part of their internal workflow. From your perspective, you have officially started building your MVP.

As the development team is working on the sprint, you will have some free time to focus on other aspects of your side venture. You can add more items to the project management tool to get ahead of the next sprint, continue to get feedback from potential customers and users, and work on your sales and marketing plan. If you have a cofounder, you can discuss your go-to-market strategy, finances, and competitors.

Meanwhile, you will come up with new feature ideas—which you can add as backlog items to the project management tool, but be careful of scope creep and derailing your MVP. This is a common problem, especially with first-time entrepreneurs. The most dangerous thing that can happen during this stage is having an Angel investor or family and friends investor without any experience in building a software product begin to make strong suggestions or demands about what they would like to see. You need to make sure you have set expectations, through a legal document, that their ideas and suggestions are welcome but that you and your cofounder are running point. Sticking to the MVP is very important. This will happen even after MVP, and the balance of investor pressure and your vision will always be a dance you will need to learn. I was in this situation many times, and even though I knew what the right thing to do was, I caved to investor requests multiple times. Now looking back, not a single situation ended up working and proving me wrong.

One of the keys to the agile process is its approach to communication. As part of your sprint, you will need to set up a daily fifteen-minute call with your PM and Business Analyst. The purpose of this call is to talk about daily progress, if pending decisions are holding up the development team, or anything else that would prevent the work that is planned for that day or the next day from happening. These calls are pivotal to help with troubleshooting, re-prioritizing, changing course, or providing whatever the development team needs. Based on my schedule, my daily calls were at 6:30 a.m., which was my India team's end of day, as they were planning for the next day. Once I got off the call, I had about an hour to get to any potential action items to prevent them from spilling into the day or night and potentially preventing me from getting to the action items. It is critical that you have a can-do attitude and not postpone or delay anything, as it can easily turn into a large snowball that will negatively impact your goals.

The next part of the agile process is testing. There will be continuous testing that your offshore team will do internally but, in some situations, you will be pulled in mid-sprint to test and provide feedback. Testing is such a critical step, as releasing a buggy product is basically dead on arrival, so let me give you a brief overview of the common testing methodologies and some best practices for your testing—for more in-depth reading on this topic, I have provided some additional resources at the end of this chapter.

White-box testing. This is where the tester has access to the code and has some level of understanding of how to read the code. This is the type of testing that will initially be happening internal to the offshore development firm you have hired.

Black-box testing. This type of testing is when you are not concerned about the code. It can also be referred to as functional testing. You only care to test performance, design, features, data, and anything in between to make sure they are working as intended without caring or understanding how they work. Even though your vendor will be doing this type of testing as well, this is probably where you will spend most of your testing hours when something is released to you.

When testing, you need to get into a focused mindset with no interruptions. Take a screenshot or video to visually show your offshore team what you are seeing when there are issues. This will dramatically reduce your back and forth compared to if you only relied on text or call to convey the issue. Each issue should be turned into a ticket in your project management software with as many details as possible. It can be tedious, but you must stay focused, thorough, and determined to ensure your MVP is at its highest quality possible. Do not assume users will be forgiving. You and possibly your cofounder designed the features being built, so you should know the ins and outs of how they should work. Write up test cases to help you remember how each feature should be tested. These documents can become valuable tools as your team grows. You might also discover that what you had imagined on paper doesn't work. Should this happen, instead of trying to fix it in the testing process, iteration should be part of the next sprint's planning.

User Acceptance Testing (UAT). This type of testing is performed by the client who is paying for something to be built—yourself in this instance—or testing by potential clients and users to ensure the release is accepted and approved. This is usually the last step in the process before deployment. For your situation, your UAT is very involved, so by definition, it is closer to Black-box testing. When you have potential clients, friends, and family give you feedback, this can be viewed as your UAT.

Automated testing. As you move past your MVP and your operation becomes more sophisticated, you want to find ways to automate your test cases as much as possible. There is an upfront cost, as you have to invest in tools and have developers write scripts for the identified test cases, but in the long run, it will save you a lot of time and money, not to mention saving you a lot of frustration, as humans are prone to make mistakes.

Regression testing. The type of testing that is best suited for automation is regression testing. This is when you want to make sure that building new functionality in one area of the product did not break functionality in other areas of the product. If your DevOps workflow doesn't account for flawless version control, you can find yourself in a situation where issues that got fixed on a previous release have resurfaced again. This gets discovered in regression testing. It is one of the most frustrating things to see fixed issues pop back up, and I cannot tell you how much time and money I wasted because of this—so do yourself a favor and start off doing it the right way, even if it feels like a lot of work and cost up front. You should drive the regression testing and create a checklist for the QA team. This checklist can eventually be used to automate the regression testing.

After testing in a sprint comes deployment. The deployment process of pushing code to your production or live environment is part of your DevOps workflow. Code is deployed then archived with version control practices in place. As you are building an MVP, you might not want to deploy any code to your live environment until MVP is complete. If you're deploying mobile code, you are going through Apple iOS or Google Play process and you can submit a build to both platforms and keep them in test mode. Once you are past your MVP and your operation is more sophisticated and hopefully you have users, customers, and revenue, your deployment process should be automated using Application Release Automation (ARA) tools.

Once the sprint is over, you need to have a post-mortem with your offshore development team to understand what worked, what challenges you faced, and discuss ways to make the next sprint more efficient. This is part of an improvement cycle you will get in, and it is critical to fine-tune your operation and processes. It will feel messy at first—especially if this is your first side venture—but if you focus on process improvement, it will improve quickly. Then you begin the planning process for your next sprint. This cycle never stops, and if you find product market fit and gain traction, it will only get more sophisticated, complicated, and involve more people in the process.

While you move on to the next sprint, you can't forget about what was built in the previous sprint. Continue to show people and get feedback. You will likely discover issues and bugs that maybe you missed initially. Having a maintenance process to fix bugs without derailing the current sprint is important, so make sure you discuss this with your offshore team.

There will be ups and downs, so stay nimble and ready to pivot and alter plans. But, how do you know that this is not going to end well and need to change vendors? There are many signs that indicate a poor vendor. The easiest indicator is poor or lack of communication—hopefully you already ruled this out during the RFP and evaluation process. Other signs to look out for are when sprint output becomes sloppier over time, which can be a result of resource issues that are being kept from you or when multiple sprints are drastically delayed even after multiple promises that "it is coming tomorrow." Also, be cautious of constant over-promising and then under-delivering. This might be a sign they are trying to drag on the project as long as possible to collect more payment, or they know they will not be able to complete it to your satisfaction. Not being able to stick to regularly scheduled calls and feeling like you need to constantly chase to get updates or for the PM to update the project management tool is a clear sign of poor skills and, when elevating your concerns to management is not met with a sense of urgency, your project might not be a priority for them.

These are just a few things to look out for, but if something doesn't feel right, most likely it is not, and you should look to move your project as soon as possible. Which, if you have done everything I have outlined, it will be a lot less painful of a process for you.

Visit the below link for a chapter summary and resources related to this chapter.

www.ch12resources.sideadventure.com

CHAPTER 13

BRANDING, MARKETING, AND SALES

"The last 10 percent it takes to launch
something takes as much energy as the first 90
percent."
Rob Kalin

"Your brand is what people say about you
after you leave the room."
Jeff Bezos, Amazon

World-renowned experts have written plenty of books about branding, marketing, and sales—you can find the best ones listed at the end of this chapter. There are seminars, classes, and coaches that focus exclusively on these topics, even if the advice and best practices change by industry, trend, and with new technology. If your corporate job touches any of these topics, you have a leg up and real-life experience you can draw on, but branding, sales, and marketing for a product and company that is in its infancy is different than for a medium- to large-size corporation. That is why in this chapter I'm going to limit my focus on what these three topics mean to me in relation to a very early stage startup that is still building an MVP.

If you are not working in or have not studied these three disciplines, when you think branding, the first thing that might come to mind is a pretty logo. When you think of marketing you probably think of some kind of advertising—such as a TV commercial or Facebook ad. When you think about sales, you probably get an image of a sleazy car salesman in your head. Let me tell you that if this is what you think of when thinking about these three aspects of business, you are wrong.

On my first few failed attempts to build a product, I put little focus on these three aspects of business at the MVP stage. I thought if I build it, they will come. Boy was I wrong! I would look at my desktop monitor and say "this looks good" or "this doesn't look good." This is how a consumer makes a design and creative decision, but if you ask them to break it down as to why, they can't, and at the time I couldn't either. I would come up with elaborate marketing ideas without having any knowledge of how to execute them. I would fantasize about having a billboard on Sunset Boulevard. I didn't realize that was more for me at a personal level to tell the world "I built this" instead of keeping the focus on the company. And when it came down to sales, it was not something I spent serious time on, as I never got to the stage with the product to try to sell it—even though I had no idea at the time that the demos and conversations I was having were in fact sales.

The good part about failing is that you learn and grow. When I was finally able to raise money to pursue the hospitality side venture, I thought I was more prepared for branding, marketing, and sales than I actually was. Since we had the funds, I took branding more seriously, but still did not follow the basics. We eventually paid a branding expert thousands of dollars for a branding exercise to help us rebrand the company, but in reality, we were branding it for the first time. This was an eye-opening experience where I learned about branding from an industry expert, but I will admit, what I learned was not earth-shattering and we did not have to spend thousands of dollars to get the results and knowledge we received.

It took much longer than I wanted to get our product ready for launch. I did not call it an MVP because scope creep dramatically made the product much bigger than it needed to be. Pressure from investors forced new functionality on the launch roadmap. As we spoke to potential customers, we heard their pain points and immediately had ideas for adding a feature or two that would solve that specific problem. We were also coming up with ideas on our own that we thought were important for launch and, as CEO, I did not do a good enough job pre-launch to manage expectations.

But once we were ready for launch, we had an amazing product. I was so proud. We were all so proud, but because it took us longer than planned to launch, we had competitors that got to market before us with a much slimmer product. We knew we were better and we wanted to get the word out fast, which is what brought us to the decision of hiring a PR firm. After spending tens of thousands of dollars with this PR firm getting the word out to the press, running marketing campaigns, and doing activation events, we were not seeing the results we wanted, so we fired the PR firm. In parallel, we attempted social media ads, formed partnerships, and ran our own marketing campaigns, but because we weren't throwing the kitchen sink at these from a monetary perspective, results were positive but slow.

We didn't have a sales team, so I took it upon myself to be our own sales team. My strategy was to sell our product by showing our potential customers what problems we could solve for them. This is when we started getting our early traction. No fancy PR firm and marketing campaign can replace getting your hands dirty and selling—especially when you are building an MVP and trying to find product market fit.

What you have to be careful of is that potential customers and users will give you feature ideas and make it seem like if you had just that one more feature, they would be a customer or user. Don't fall into the trap of chasing features because you believe that will lead to a sale. If a person is not willing to use your MVP, adding another feature won't make a difference unless you had a research and development team with a multi-million-dollar budget that developed something so novel that sets you above all your competitors. The reality is that you don't have an R&D department, and any new feature you build your competitors can easily replicate as well. If your potential customers and users are sold on your MVP but need a few more features, they should become a customer first before you go off and spend time and money to build additional functionality that you have no idea if it will benefit anyone else.

So, what is branding, marketing, and sales for an early-stage startup from my perspective?

Branding. Just as people have reputations, so do companies and products. The experience you offer consumers is your brand. Branding is how you give your company its own voice, beliefs, identity, story, and personality—how you differentiate from your competitors.

For startups that are bootstrapping to build their MVP and for entrepreneurs that are brand-new or still early in their entrepreneurship journey, it's common to put all the focus on the logo or other tangible assets when you think about branding. I sure did. Your goal at the MVP stage is to find product market fit and prove to investors you have a viable product and a business model that will build a profitable company. Because of this, the brand of your startup starts with you. It's your story and why you set out on this venture to begin with, so the first step in your branding exercise is to write a short bio of yourself. Where did you grow up? What is your academic background? What is your professional background? What inspires you? What are your aspirations? What led you to pursue this side venture? What good would you like to achieve with your side venture? This in essence becomes the early identity and voice of your startup.

This is not in sequential order, as you have probably thought about your company name long before you started your side venture, but a good name is the next important factor in your branding exercise. Your company name should be short and sweet. I prefer a name that is one or two syllables, but that does not mean names with more than two syllables are automatically rejected. Apple, Uber, Google, and Facebook are one- or two-syllable names, but Instagram and Amazon are amazing names that are more than two syllables.

In addition, your company name should be easy to pronounce and easy to spell. You should think as global as possible to make expansion into new markets easier. Speaking of expansion, your name should be broad enough to allow you to expand into other areas. Amazon is the perfect case study for this. Jeff Bezos wanted to sell every book possible, and the name "Amazon" allowed the brand to do this, which is a play on the Amazon jungle, an area that contains the highest diversity of wildlife on Earth. At the same time, the name allowed Amazon to easily expand into other product types to fulfill its brand promise of being the "Everything Store," which was all part of its strategy from its early days. To protect your brand, you don't want a name that has any negative connotations. From a legal standpoint, you want a name you can trademark, and most importantly, you want to be unique.

In previous chapters, we talked about your mission and vision for your company and identifying the problem you are trying to solve and why. Now you can take your mission to the next level by drafting your mission statement and purpose. The mission statement has the opportunity to be the foundation of your company's culture and help guide everyone towards the same goal. Amazon's mission statement is "To be Earth's most customer-centric company; to build a place where people can come to find and discover anything they might want to buy online." You can see how this statement penetrates the DNA of its employees and guides what they do and how they do it. Let's look at another example. Google's mission statement is "To organize the world's information and make it universally accessible and useful." Similar to Amazon, Google's mission statement points the employees and management in the same direction. Your mission statement should be simple and use the bare minimum number of words to describe what your company is striving to do. This becomes the purpose of why your company exists, and you need a purpose you truly believe in to push you through the tough times—especially when quitting feels easier than moving forward.

The next step is to design your logo, but to do this you need to think about colors and fonts. Given that most early-stage startups are strapped for cash, you'll be using one of the freelance communities to design your logo. That is what I did but, given my lack of knowledge on logo design, I wasn't able to provide the right direction to the artists I had hired. Instead, I chose some logos I liked and told the artists, "This is what I like. Design a logo in this style using my company name." This is not a good approach, as the goal of a logo is to be unique and memorable, not look like other logos.

You can study colors for a whole career, as each color has meaning and emotion associated with it and they can change over time and be different based on culture. You don't have that kind of time, so the quick and simple approach is to start writing down the emotions you want people to feel when they use your product or think of your company. Once you've decided on four or five words, Google which colors are associated with these emotions and then select two or three colors you want your brand to be associated with. You can do similar research with fonts. In addition, because you have already done a competitive analysis, you should know what your competitors are doing, and you want to make sure you don't come across as a copycat.

This will give your designer the information they need to begin formulating ideas for you. You will go through several iterations—focus on simplicity and uniqueness. Also, you need to think about how your logo converts into an app icon if you have a mobile product. Ask your designer for several combinations on different backgrounds and different platforms, like a business card, website header, and anywhere else you can image your logo, so you can see how it translates. Even if your heart is set on a single design, make sure you get feedback from friends, family, and potential users and customers to see if how they describe the logo maps back to your mission, purpose, and the emotions you wanted people to feel.

Before finishing, you need to master your one-line pitch. At the early stages, your one-line pitch will become your most important weapon in a conversation with anyone about your side venture—especially investors. Your one-line pitch must be short and describe the problem you are solving, not what the company does. If your parents or grandparents can't understand it, then it's either using industry-specific terminology that most people don't understand or it's too vague.

At the end of this process, you will document all your work into a style guide—I have provided you with a list of tools at the end of this chapter. The tool I have used the most recently is Frontify. The style guide will help you with the look and feel for every touchpoint your company and product will have with consumers, investors, and employees. Without going through the most basics of a branding exercise, your marketing campaigns can turn into a huge waste of time and money, your pitch decks can look sloppy, and your employees will have a hard time rallying around you. Keep in mind that your style guide will be a living document, as you will have to adapt and change as you grow, and being able to quickly communicate to employees, vendors, and contractors will be critical to keep consistency at all times.

Marketing. Marketing is the process and all activities associated with generating interest, finding leads, and selling a product or service. It includes market research, promotions and advertising, selling and the delivery, and customer experience of the product or service.

It is a massive topic and, as I mentioned earlier, there are many books, articles, workshops, and seminars that go deep into teaching marketing—not to mention academic disciplines that focus on it as well. My intent in this chapter is not to go deep but touch on some key things you need to focus on to launch your MVP.

Instead of marketing, you should be planning your go-to-market strategy, which is marketing for a startup at the MVP stage. A go-to-market strategy is how you plan to get your initial customer or users and how you will leverage the process to attain product market fit. This should be your only goal. It doesn't matter how elaborate your marketing concepts are, what partnerships you have formed, how many social media followers you have attracted, or that maybe you have a marketing background and specialize in SEO, social media marketing, email marketing, or another media type. If you don't have a product or service that your intended target demographic wants, none of it matters. That is why your only goal with your go-to-market strategy and any marketing you do is to validate or iterate until you have product market fit. Let's talk about some of the steps in this process.

You might not consciously have known, but all the feedback you have been gathering through every step in the process was the start of your go-to-market strategy. Since your goal is to have a product that finds product market fit, the primary aspect of your go-to-market strategy starts in the engineering and product design process. You need to make sure your product works right, fast, and solves the single problem you intended to solve, incorporates valid feedback, and finally, you are thinking about building virality and marketing hooks directly into the product.

What do I mean by virality or marketing hooks built directly into your product? Also known as growth hacking, this is where, either intentionally or unintentionally, your customers and users spread the message of the existence of your product with social proof that they are using the product, which acts as positive word-of-mouth marketing. This is the best type of marketing, as there is no incremental cost, and fans of your product are doing the work, which can lead to exponential growth.

One classic example of growth hacking is Hotmail. When Hotmail launched in 1996 as one of the early free email services, to get the word out, the Hotmail team added the link "PS: I love you. Get your free email at Hotmail" at the bottom of every email sent. Clicking on the link sent you to the Hotmail registration page. By turning users of Hotmail into word-of-mouth marketers, Hotmail grew exponentially, and on December 31, 1997, Microsoft acquired Hotmail for $500 million. Other examples are YouTube allowing its videos to be embedded on websites or Facebook allowing users to import their email contact list so you can easily invite your contacts to Facebook. Every product is unique, and if the product is a software as a service (SaaS) product, the strategies and approach will be different. The only common denominator is that you need to build a product that is worth talking about, then make it super simple and easy for your customers and users to talk about—even if they don't know they are, like in the Hotmail example.

By the time you begin the development of your MVP, you should have gathered a lot of feedback from friends, family, and potential users and customers. But to attain product market fit and create a viable business that generates profit, you need feedback from early adopters. This means you have to build the feedback loop into your product. It can be automated emails or built into the product experience, but it needs to be simple, fast, and the data easily converted into action items. No matter the industry you are entering, being customer-focused is always a winning strategy, but being obsessed with listening to your early adopters can be the difference between success and failure. You want to understand your customer and user journey through every part of your product and simplify when possible. Instagram started as a location-sharing platform, but as the founders of Instagram tracked how users were engaging with the product, they realized the photo functionality was what was being used the most, so they simplified the product to focus on photo sharing and renamed the product "Instagram." There are various services you can use to track engagement within your product to make data-driven decisions on what is being used and what is not. I have provided some resources on this at the end of this chapter.

You can also employ marketing channels to collect feedback during your development process and master your ideal customer profile, such as using Facebook ads for a data-driven approach to understand your potential early adopters. Once you get into post-MVP-launch marketing, understanding your ideal customer profile will be critical—otherwise, you will see dollars wasted on leads and targets that do not need your product.

For example, you can create a landing page that asks for an email address, using various Facebook ads to drive traffic to this landing page, and then measure conversion. You can also create an ad targeted at different demographics and measure engagement within Facebook without any additional effort. This only requires an understanding of how Facebook ads work. You can also use the various social network advertising platforms to fine-tune your messaging and images you are contemplating using. For instance, you can create various Instagram ads with different images you have selected coupled with the tagline options you are trying to decide on and see which ones get you the most engagement. Quora and Reddit are also great platforms to get feedback.

As I have focused so much on feedback, I want to make sure you don't consider feedback as something a person does or says. Feedback is any type of data that you can leverage to move toward product market fit. You can do split testing to see if sign-up form A is more effective than sign-up form B. You can use services where you pay people to act as customers or users and use your product and give you feedback. You can also embed code into your product to track how users navigate within your product to understand engagement and behavior.

Once you launch your MVP, based on the data-driven success criteria you have established, you will know if you have reached product market fit. To do this, you have to identify what paid media channels are best for your company, as each channel requires its own specialized knowledge and expertise. We hired experts for the channels that we felt were appropriate for our product.

Search Engine Optimization (SEO). By optimizing and testing keywords the general public searches for, you can drive organic traffic to your product. The techniques and skills needed evolve quickly, as Google and other search engines regularly update their algorithms, so trying to do this as a generalist will probably not get you the results you are looking for.

Email Marketing. Even though it is considered an older channel, it is still effective if done correctly. You can use services like ConstentContact or any other similar service to run your email campaigns, but there is a catch. With anti-spam laws in every country, the email addresses you use must be from people who voluntarily provided you their email and have opted in to receive emails from you.

Social Media Marketing. As the name suggests, this involves using Facebook, Instagram, Twitter, TikTok, LinkedIn, or any other social media platform to advertise. The basic idea is the same across all platforms, but they differ in execution and use cases. You must understand each platform's strengths and weaknesses, learn their advertising platform, and have a strategy in place before starting to spend your budget.

Paid Media Marketing. This type of advertising is most likely not something you'd want to do early in your startup. TV commercials, radio ads, and billboards might sound exciting, but you need to be lean and focus on ROI. This type of marketing is expensive and takes a lot of effort to execute. The only type of paid media advertising that might make sense for you is banner advertising through Google, Facebook, or any other digital ad platform. But just like social media marketing, you need to understand how these platforms work and have a strategy in place before spending a dime.

Owned Media Marketing. This refers to channels you own—your company's social media accounts, blog, and website. To generate followers or readers of your blog is no small task. It's similar to treating them as sub-products that require their own marketing effort.

Influencer Marketing. Because it takes time and effort to build up a following on social media, many companies and brands turn to influencer marketing. Influencers are people that have put in a lot of time and effort to build a social media following and can in return push a product or service to their followers. There are now agencies and online services that can help you connect with influencers that have followers in the demographic you are targeting.

Affiliate Marketing. With this type of marketing, you pay a third party to drive traffic to your product and you pay a commission based on your terms. There are various affiliate marketing platforms you can use to engage in this type of marketing. The key here is having your style guide ready so the third party is representing your brand accurately, as they will leverage various channels to promote your product or service at their own expense. Because you are not in control, the risk is that your brand may not be represented as you would like. The affiliate marketer is incentivized in getting paid their commission, not maintaining your brand image, so use this type of marketing only when it makes sense.

Press. Getting any type of positive press coverage is great for a startup. You can draft a press kit and email journalists and bloggers, but at the end of the day, if you want press coverage you need to have a product and company worth talking about. Journalists are inundated with press kits, so they are looking for compelling stories to write about. I also don't recommend hiring a PR firm in the early stages, as a PR firm will not improve your product.

Trade Shows. As soon as you can, you should start attending trade shows within your industry as a visitor. Not only will it help you keep a pulse on your industry, but you can also see what incumbent and potential new competitors might be working on. It will also help you be better prepared for when you decide to be an exhibitor and use the trade show to market and sell your product.

Partnerships. This form of marketing can be very lucrative for early-stage startups, as you form a partnership with another brand as a business development opportunity that creates value for both sides. This comes down to finding the right partner and your ability to sell your idea.

To increase the chance of success for your marketing campaign, using any of the channels, you need to do a few things. First, you need to be clear on your campaign objectives. Are you trying to get 1000 pre-launch emails that will fill up your lead pipeline? Are you trying to test your slogan? Be clear on the objective so you know how to determine success and failure. Second, since you have created the ideal customer profile, start thinking about the emotional side of this ideal customer. Your ability to put yourself in their shoes will help you understand how to tap into their emotion to get them to take your desired action. And third, with every marketing channel and campaign, if you are not measuring your success, you will be driving blind. Marketing performance metrics will tell you with data if something is working or not. What data is used to measure performance will vary based on the channel and platform, so you need to study your selected channel. For example, Facebook will provide you with engagement metrics that show how many Facebook users engaged with your ad.

Before you embark on any major marketing campaigns, you must have a marketing plan. This is the document that outlines your marketing activities and the strategies you need to implement to achieve the desired objectives. It will include the work you have already done identifying the problem you are trying to solve and the need you are fulfilling, your ideal customer profile, an analysis of the current market conditions, and the competitor landscape with a detailed project plan with specific tasks, goals, objectives, and your budget. You need a marketing plan to act as your map, set deadlines, and understand what it is you are trying to accomplish over the next six to twelve months—otherwise, it will turn into an unorganized web of activities that do not come together, wasting time and money. This will be the focus of the person managing marketing on your team. Having someone with experience in this will make a huge difference.

Now let's talk about sales. Even though it can fall under a broader marketing strategy, it is its own giant topic.

Sales. This refers to the activities that lead to the selling of a good or service. This is the generic definition of sales, but sales are also influence. Sales are communication. Sales mean convincing a guy or gal to go on a date with you. Sales mean building relationships. Depending on if you are building a B2C or B2B product, your approach to sales will be different, especially if your B2C product is a free product—like Instagram—which you plan to monetize in different ways once you have hit critical mass adoption. No matter what product you are building, you need to completely change how you think about sales, especially if you have negative connotations toward the word. Getting friends and family to give you feedback on your idea is sales. Getting early users and potential customers to provide you with feedback is sales. Convincing anyone to give you money to pursue your side venture is sales.

For a B2C product, as soon as you get into the process of talking about the problem you are trying to solve, capturing regular feedback at every stage of the process, being hands-on with your early users to understand what is working and what is not working, and every demo you do to showcase your product to your target demographic, you are selling. Not to mention demos for investors. To be able to do this, you need marketing to support your sales. This includes branding, consistency in all touchpoints, and how you describe your product. In most cases, B2C startups don't need a sales team in the early stages as the founders are the sales team. The same is true for B2B products, but there is a lot more to the selling process since you will be asking for payment in exchange for your product. The rest of this chapter is more focused on startups building a B2B product, but it is also relevant to B2C startups as well.

The most challenging part of a startup is finding your first five to ten customers that are willing to pay you. It is scary, daunting, and it will feel like more failure than success early on. At this early stage, the trick is to find customers that understand how to work with a startup, are willing to take a chance on a product that is unproven in the market, and can deal with technical issues—technical issues will happen no matter how well you tested the product. At this stage, you are more in the customer discovery process than hard sales.

Having a customer that is aligned with your goals makes them a partner, even though they are paying you for your product. And a partner, by definition, will help you prove your product and assumptions in actual day-to-day usage instead of just test scenarios. This is exactly what I did in the last startup we took a product to market. Our first three customers became our partners, and with their help, we made feedback-driven iterations. I would visit their office multiple times during the week, sit next to employees, and watch them use the product. I would ask them questions to solicit feedback. This is why, for the early sales, it is always best to be done by the founders, as they understand the product better than anyone and can speak about the company in the right way. A hands-on approach like this is time-consuming, but I find it a must-do to get to product market fit. The other benefit is that it allows you to build relationships, and as employees and executives move around to other companies in the same industry, a positive relationship can lead to sales as well. In reverse, if the founders are not able to sell the product, then it is unlikely professional salespeople can generate repeatable sales. A founder's ability to sell is also something an experienced investor will look for.

Before you get in front of a qualified lead, you need a pricing strategy. This is an area many first-time entrepreneurs struggle with, mainly because they do not have enough internal data and are going off of competitive analysis and external data. The common mistake from only relying on external data is that you end up setting a price too low or too high or establish a complicated pricing model that is hard to explain. Instead, the better approach is to use external data coupled with the feedback you have been capturing during your pre-MVP launch process.

When speaking with potential customers, focus on feedback on the problem statement and the product, and learn about their business. If you have put in the effort to build a relationship, you will be able to ask them about their budget and how much they are paying for other software services or paying for the software that your product might be replacing. This type of conversation with three to five leads during your pre-MVP launch process will help you establish a go-to-market pricing strategy.

In the marketing section of this chapter, I emphasized the importance of understanding and creating the ideal customer profile. One of the areas where that exercise will become beneficial is identifying leads. Your initial leads might be introductions made by a mutual party, but the more common approach to generating leads is using the various marketing channels we discussed earlier. Depending on your industry, you can also buy leads, but that can become a large expense. It is also not suitable for a startup in the MVP stage, as you won't be able to handle a large number of leads anyway.

Irrespective of which channel you use to generate leads, what is important is that you capture the data and measure success by the use of metrics that can be used in conjunction with your marketing metrics. There is robust Customer Relationship Management (CRM) software off the shelf—like Salesforce—that will allow you to capture information about a lead and assist with follow-ups and moving the lead through the sales funnel. These types of tools can be great when you are operating at scale with a sales team but, at the MVP stage, I used Google Sheets, as it was faster and did not have a learning curve. From a sales perspective and at a high level, some of the metrics you want to capture are leads per marketing channel, leads per day, conversion rate, and closing rate. Also, by understanding average sale size, how long it takes to take a customer from lead to a close, and how many leads are in the pipeline, you can begin forecasting future revenue, which will become the basis for raising funds during your growth phase.

If you have not worked in sales, I can share with you a simple process you can follow to take a lead to close. If you have a simple product with simple pricing available on your website where a customer can use the information to make a buy decision, this is considered an automated sale. The effort here is more on the marketing channels and driving leads to your website. The human involvement to go from lead to close is for either outside or inside sales. Outside sales are when you or a salesperson meet qualified leads in person. This is time-consuming and expensive since travel is involved, but might be your best option if it is a lucrative deal. Inside sales refer to selling from the office or remotely where conversations are via phone or video calls and the demo of the product is virtual.

Once a lead has been identified through a marketing channel, you now have to qualify the lead. This means scheduling that initial conversation to understand if they meet your criteria for becoming a customer. You should have a script to stay consistent with the questions you ask to understand the lead's problems and their appetite for buying your product, how you will talk about the product and the company, and how you will talk about pricing. Be ready to turn negatives into positives. At the end of the day, a lead is qualified if they truly are in the market for a product like yours. Trying to convince a "No, I'm not interested" to "Yes, I'm interested" is not the responsibility of sales. Responsibility of sales is to take the "Yes, I'm interested" through a smooth process of becoming a customer, and for leads that are a "maybe" to provide accurate and honest information and squash rejections to see if they become a "Yes" or a "No." In short, you ask them questions to identify your lead's problems and how this makes them feel, then gain their trust to offer your product as the solution.

The next step in the process will be to demo and follow up. You want a demo that speaks to your qualified lead. If possible, customize the demo so your qualified lead sees data and images relevant to their company. You want the demo to be sharp, have no technical issues, and only cover primary functionality that your lead is interested in. This is something you should have captured during your lead qualification conversation. Don't spend an hour going through every page and all the scenarios. You should have your user journey already mapped out, so take your lead through the journey so they can connect the dots instead of jumping from one feature to another. If there is a contract involved, you might want to consider sending them the contract after the demo. You might be asked to schedule multiple demos, so be prepared by understanding the audience in advance.

The last step is to close the sale. This is where you are reiterating that your product will solve their problem and answering additional questions. There will likely be multiple follow-ups in the closing process, as other departments like legal or operations might now be involved, so you have to stay patient and persistent. This will for sure be the case if you are dealing with a large corporation, as even IT security teams will have to get involved. If you have come this far, it is most likely because the qualified lead is sold on your product but is dealing with internal matters. Taking the time to build a relationship and showing your dependability will go a long way, but as I mentioned before, do not get stuck in the trap of building new functionality because of a request to close. And as part of the close, make sure you quickly take care of the contract and get the appropriate signature to memorialize the agreement. As you go through the lead qualification to the closing process, there are some best practices you can use to improve your chances.

Sell the benefits, not the features. This is a common mistake first-time entrepreneurs make. You have designed the features and understand exactly how they work and why they are beneficial, so you lead in with the features. They are in your pitch deck, website's home page, and in your app description. Your lead will be more interested in the benefits. How does your product benefit their company and also, how does it benefit the individual? Does it save the company $200,000 a year, which the individual lead can use to advance their own career? Your marketing material should lead with benefits. You will fine-tune this when you are having your early conversations.

Be clear and concise on what you are offering. This only happens when you master your elevator pitch and understand the problem you are trying to solve. Use everyday words, and if your product has multiple user types, don't go into the weeds of trying to explain the benefit to each user type. Understand your audience and speak to their needs.

Focus on the decision-maker. Related to the above, you need to impress the buyer even if they will not be the everyday user of your product. Maybe the decision-maker is an executive and they are only interested in a monthly report. Understand the decision-maker's needs and incorporate their needs into your demo and pitch.

Storytelling. This is the most powerful tool in any type of communication, especially in sales. Stories will draw and keep your audience's attention. Tell the story of how the company started, a story that makes the problem statement feel real and human. If possible, the story of how a previous customer has benefited from your product. A dry presentation might get the job done, but a presentation with stories will be remembered. Stories touch the heart, and when stories touch the heart, closing the sale becomes a lot easier.

Be authentic. Don't try to represent your company and product as something it is not. Trying to act like a big company and over-promising will eventually backfire. Be honest and authentic. Remember, the people taking a chance on a startup are essentially taking a chance on the founders, so they want to know they are working with people that have high integrity.

As you go through this process, know that you will fail many times and you will hear a lot more "No" than "Yes." Embrace the failures and learn from them. Entrepreneurship is about determination, resilience, and endurance. It's a marathon, not a hundred-meter dash. Let the failures motivate you to prove people wrong. Have the conviction that you deserve success in life, and if your product or service does not find product market fit, bring all the knowledge and experience you've acquired to your next one. You are always one idea away from success.

Visit the below link for a chapter summary and resources related to this chapter.

www.ch13resources.sideadventure.com

CHAPTER 14

FUNDRAISING

"The best entrepreneurs are not the best
visionaries. The greatest entrepreneurs are
incredible salespeople. They know how to tell
an amazing story that will convince talent and
investors to join in on the journey."
Alejandro Cremades

"Fundraising is an extreme sport!" Marc A.
Pitman

I'm a true believer that you need to start your venture with
your own money to prove to yourself and others that you
have what it takes to build a prototype. If you take money
from friends and family to get started and then lose it, not only
will you lose credibility, and the ability to raise more money
from the same friends and family, but you might also damage
your relationships.

For my first handful of failed attempts, I spent thousands
of dollars from my savings to build the prototypes. Even though
they were failures, I was able to prove to myself and to friends
and family that I could turn an idea into reality. I also realized
that I truly loved the process, which was key in not giving up. I
got better with each attempt, and instead of looking at the side
ventures as failures and money lost, I viewed each failure as

experience and wisdom and the cost associated with each as an investment into the next side venture. This mindset was critical, as fear and failure were blocked out of my head.

Once I got to my successful hospitality side venture, Michael knew I was not all talk, which is why he wanted in. So, we started this venture with the both of us putting in 50 percent of the estimated cost to build a prototype and getting the venture off the ground. Even as a prototype, this was the most complex product to date I had tackled as a side venture. It was late 2009 when we started going through the process of building the prototype. The third-generation iPhone had just launched, and the Apple App Store and the Google Play App Store had been around for less than eighteen months. By the time we had an aspect of our prototype to look at and test, the first-generation Samsung Galaxy S had released. Smart mobile devices and mobile apps dominated the tech news landscape, so it was clear to me that mobile was the future and that if we wanted to be successful with our prototype, we had to demonstrate how our product would go mobile as well.

Like any new technology, the number of people skilled and educational content on the new technology were limited but I set my mind on understanding mobile apps and the cost to build a prototype. After hours of reading, watching videos, and sending emails to experts, I had enough of an understanding and was able to draw on paper what our prototype mobile app would look like, what functionalities it would include, and how it would be an extension of the website to solve the problem we were intending to solve.

After getting a few cost estimates, it was clear that anything to do with mobile was still considered a premium and we could not fund it ourselves. While the desktop prototype was moving forward slowly, I shifted my focus to coming up with ideas on how to raise money. Family was out of the question, but I was able to raise a few thousand dollars from friends with whom I had established credibility over the years. But I knew it wasn't enough, so I started talking about what we were trying to do with anyone that would listen. Talking to people about our side venture also allowed us to not only get feedback and validate the problem statement but also work on our elevator pitch.

During the days, I was focused on my corporate job but during nights, weekends, and any free time I had, I was singularly focused on raising money. I couldn't think about anything else, and the universe knew my intentions. I was focused on Angel investors, as I knew we were too early for any type of VC funding. I also knew that accelerator programs would not be an option either, as we did not think it was the right time to quit our jobs. This was late 2010 and we were in the midst of the Great Recession. I would even talk to people that I knew were not investors but perhaps knew one.

I cannot emphasize the importance of building a genuine and positive relationship as the primary goal. Without this type of relationship, no one will be willing to stick their neck out for you and make introductions. This has been my philosophy for as long as I can remember. I never expect anything in return right away from a relationship. I believe that the universe puts people in our lives for a reason, and as long as I do my part to be a genuinely good person and add something positive to their life, over time the reason why a person is in my life will be revealed to me.

With this mindset, I kept going, and after months it finally happened. I was in Las Vegas for a conference related to my corporate job—it was also my birthday; what better place to be on your birthday than Las Vegas, right? But I was by myself with no plans. Since the side venture was in hospitality, we had been networking and had numerous acquaintances in Las Vegas, and a few of them had become good friends. One of them found out

I was in Las Vegas and that it was my birthday. They sent me a text message inviting me to dinner and told me that a person I had briefly met a couple of months before was also attending the same dinner and was insisting I join them. I ended up going, and a great dinner that did not include any business talk led to going to a party at XS at the Wynn. The person I had briefly met a couple of months before pulled me aside inside the nightclub and told me that he had heard about the project I was working on and that he was interested in what we were trying to do. As you can imagine, the music was loud—not the best environment for me to rattle off my elevator pitch—so I suggested that once I got back home, I would email him details and a link to the prototype.

The combination of having credibility with a friend that was willing to stick their neck out for me, coming across as likable, responsible, and genuine, and demonstrating execution ability in the form of a prototype led to getting a large check a few weeks after that initial email. This jumpstarted the product and led to a true friendship with the person that believed in me. Part of the adventure is the relationships you build and the memories you create that no-one can take away from you.

Raising funds beyond family and friends for first-time unproven entrepreneurs can feel like a daunting task and black box, especially if you were in my shoes and did not have a network of multi-millionaires. There also isn't a one-size-fits-all playbook that is guaranteed to work all the time, so it takes resilience, persistence, and thick skin, as you will directly or indirectly hear ninety-nine "No's" before you get the one "Yes." Similar to the chapter on branding, marketing, and sales, while I will brush the different types of funding, the focus of this chapter will be seed funding, which is typically before MVP or as you plan your go-to-market strategy.

Raising funds for an unproven product is difficult. You are selling the promise of tomorrow and what success can look like, and getting that first investor on board can feel like climbing Mount Everest. You have been working on branding, your story, and your elevator pitch, now it's time to sell to investors. This is why sales is such an important part of a founder's role. Investors want to see that you are focused, understand the problem statement that you are selling them on, and that it is a big enough problem to build a company around.

A seed investor is investing in you and your founding team as much as they are investing in the product. Experienced investors know that it is likely you will pivot from the original idea as you gather more data and feedback. The earlier in the venture you try to raise money, the higher the risks are for the investor, which will result in the investor asking for more equity in the company and potentially negotiating terms that put them in a more favorable place compared to subsequent investors. Seed investors also want to see the money go toward product development and your go-to-market strategy instead of salaries and office space.

It takes a lot of effort to raise money, and it can become a distraction from building the product, so you want to be sure that you have gone as far as you can with either self-funding or a friends and family round. I have mentioned "seed round" several times, but just to familiarize you with the various rounds of funding, let's go over each one. There are varying definitions depending on who you talk to and what material you read, but they boil down to the following.

Friends and Family. Obviously, this is when you raise funding from friends and family. Because of the built-in relationship, they are an easy and familiar source. Typical friends and family funding is a few thousand dollars to $100,000, but just because they are friends and family and not disciplined investors, does not mean you should not take the same care in preparing your pitch and presentation. Don't take their money just because they want to help, as this can have a negative impact. In addition, money raised from friends and family should be memorialized and treated with the appropriate legal backdrop to prevent issues further down the line that can impact your future funding rounds.

Seed. Sometimes referred to as series A or Angel round, this is when you have a prototype or an MVP and need funding to prove your concept and establish product market fit. Investors for this round are individual accredited investors—typically known as Angel investors. The SEC defines an accredited investor as an individual who has a net worth of at least one million dollars and an annual income of at least $200,000 or $300,000 jointly with a spouse. They are taking a big risk betting on you with their personal finances at this very early stage, so they will be looking to acquire a meaningful part of your company in the form of equity in addition to asking for some favorable terms in the agreement. As an example, specific voting rights like key hiring decisions or who is put on the company board of directors. Common seed rounds are from $50,000 to a couple of million, but be aware that an Angel might commit to investing one million dollars, but you won't be getting a check for one million. To protect themselves, the Angel investor will release funds slowly as you hit key milestones and metrics.

Venture Capital (VC). Venture capitalists are usually private or public companies that professionally manage the money of wealthy individuals or organizations who are paid to generate a return on their client's investment. A very small percentage of companies successfully raise VC money, as the criteria is very narrow for each firm, but one common criterion is a company that is generating revenue and is at the very early stages of exponential growth that is backed by data. VC funding can be from low millions to billions, as VC funding can happen in several rounds as well. On top of capital to grow the company, VCs provide invaluable insight, can seed the company with managerial experience, and can connect founders to other successful founders.

Accelerator. Accelerators and incubators are organizations usually made up of serial entrepreneurs or investors that are now trying to use their experience and network to help early-stage companies develop their idea. Entrepreneurs accepted into an accelerator program will share space with other entrepreneurs where the rate of learning and feedback can be accelerated, leading to an increase in the speed of getting an MVP out to market. Accelerators are very selective, and each organization will tend to specialize in a specific industry. An accelerator also has strict rules and requirements, which makes it a difficult option if anyone starts out with a side venture.

Crowdfunding. This is a more recent and innovative mode to raise funding, popularized by companies like Kickstarter. The concept is simple: Instead of one or two Angel investors, you post your project on a platform and individual users agree to fund the project in exchange for discounts and other perks the company offers instead of equity. This is because, before 2016, it was not legal to allow just anyone to buy equity in private companies. In 2016, the Title III Job Act was signed into law, which changed this, giving birth to companies like Republic that enable anyone to invest as little as $10 in a private company. For both scenarios, funds are released only when you have met your funding goal. It takes a lot of effort to get a crowdfunding campaign off the ground and it might restrict you from future funding, so do your research for your specific scenario before deciding to go this route.

Initial Public Offering (IPO). The holy grail for most entrepreneurs is either a large exit or an IPO. An IPO is when you move your company from being a private entity to a public entity where shares are traded publicly on Wall Street or an equivalent stock market. This is an extremely complicated process, with major banks and law firms hired to put everything together, and the founders go on roadshows to sell investment bankers and hedge funds to buy into the IPO.

Before you start contacting prospective investors, you need to make sure you have all your ducks in order, which means having a killer investors sales pitch. This is the main tool in your quest to raise funding. All the work you have already done to understand your industry and customers, the problem you are trying to solve, and how you will build a business model around your product will come together in your pitch deck. There are steps you can take to improve your chances.

First, tell a story. Don't get into a boring pitch with graphs and financial data without a narrative linking it all together. Stories are how you will pull in your audience's attention, and once you get their attention, wow them with the graphs and data.

Make sure you cater your pitch to your prospective investor. Doing your research to understand your audience will result in a pitch that speaks to them and highlights what they care about the most, thus increasing your chances of a yes. If your prospect is more interested in seeing your prototype, don't spend forty-five minutes on your presentation and ten minutes on your prototype. In this instance, cut the slides short and weave your pitch into your product demo. Your sales pitch should not be more than ten to twelve pages. Keep the slides light by only including the most important part of the story being told on each slide—three to four bullet points or one or two images. The rest should be rehearsed talking points. This will convey that you know what you are talking about instead of just reading every single word.

You need to be specific about your objectives and clearly state them at the beginning of your pitch, and with each slide, demonstrate why they should invest in you. Be specific on your problem statement, your solution and intended business model, and your intended timelines for raising funding. If you have early users or partners, include testimonials and, if possible, demonstrate how they have benefited from your product. You are raising funds for a product and company that is most likely not profitable yet, so avoid detailed and exaggerated sales projections and revenue forecasts. Be transparent and honest about where your company is and be realistic about potential revenue. At this stage, the investor is betting more on the founding team than the product itself.

Always end with a call to action to guide investors to take the next step, and leave some time at the end for Q&A. As you have been going through the journey, you have probably heard most of the questions that investors will ask but in different forms. Anticipate the questions by creating a list of expected questions and rehearsing the answers. With every new question you hear, you should be adding it to the list of questions you need to rehearse for.

Throughout the entire process, be genuine and let your personality and how you want your company to be represented come through in the pitch. Don't try to act like a major corporation, because you are not. Don't go out of your character. Just be you, as the investor wants to bet on you. When it comes to the pitch deck, there isn't an industry standard, but there are some key parts you want to make sure you cover—I have provided some examples for you to use as a reference at the end of this chapter.

First, you want to use your style guide to stay on brand—which is why you went through the branding exercise. You want to start with the company logo and your mission and vision statements. Talk about your strategy for the company if you are successful. This will communicate your aspirations to the investor.

The next section should be all about your problem statement, why your product is the right solution at this moment in time, and who the intended users or customers are. Highlight key benefits of your product and include a six- to twelve-month product and company roadmap. This should include specific milestones and metrics you are trying to hit. For example, $150,000 in revenue in twelve months or 25,000 active users in six months.

Next, based on the market research and competitive analysis you have been doing, you will educate the investor on the addressable market and what is possible from a revenue standpoint. Again, avoid exaggerating and making statements like "We are the Airbnb for closets." Don't sell an unrealistic dream at this stage where you have no traction. Include your competitive analysis and any trends you have observed in the market. This will tell the investor you have a pulse on your industry and are well informed.

You then want to talk about your business model and how you intend to make money. If you already have some sales or traction with users, highlight it. This is social proof that the addressable market you have defined is actually interested in your product.

End with introducing the team, their background, and why the investor should believe in your team's ability. Restate your fundraising needs, how it will be used, and any financial projections you have. Again, do not exaggerate the projections. Always assume the investor is smarter and more knowledgeable than you are about your industry and addressable market. Sometimes, things can move very fast and you get a yes right away, so be ready to have a lawyer send a term sheet immediately.

You can also use online tools like Clerky to create your legal term sheet and other documents.

So how do you find Angel investors? It comes down to networking and putting yourself out there to meet new people. You can also attend pitchfests and take advantage of online investor communities like Anglelist and CrunchBase—check the list at the end of the chapter. If you are meeting investors in person at a networking event or at a pitchfest, don't try to throw the entire kitchen sink at the investor in the short few minutes you have. Your goal is to secure a meeting. Meeting other entrepreneurs who have received funding is also valuable, as they will be able to make referrals. Being introduced to an investor by a person the investor knows and trusts will dramatically increase your chance of landing a meeting. Cold calls and emails usually don't work unless you have something very special. For example, you have a startup focused on basketball fans and Michael Jordan has agreed to be the face of your company. There is very little chance of this happening.

If you are emailing an investor to try to set up a meeting, keep the email short and leverage your elevator pitch. Include growth metrics, if possible. Having some kind of traction will increase your chances exponentially. Be specific about your call to action, which is a meeting request, and follow up in a few days if you have not heard back. There are a million reasons why someone might have missed an email or read the email but forgot to respond. Don't automatically assume they are not interested. Also, do not share your deck or a link to your prototype or MVP at this stage. You don't want the deck being used out of context and someone not familiar with the prototype or MVP to try to figure out how to navigate it.

As you start pitching, a common question you will have to answer is company valuation. Because you are still trying to find product market fit and have zero profit, valuation becomes more art than science. This is called pre-money valuation. Once you raise your seed round, your valuation will be known as post-money valuation, meaning that an investor has given your company a value on paper. Expect seed investors to ask for 20–45 percent of the company, depending on the size of the investment. So, based on how much you have valued your company, the investment you get will be the percentage of the company the investor is buying. A seed round can be a few hundred thousand dollars—unless you are an experienced entrepreneur with a successful exit, in which case you might be able to raise two to ten million dollars, based on the market size, industry, and valuation. For your case, an experienced Angel investor knows that you will probably need more money, as inexperienced entrepreneurs don't know to plan for what they don't know.

The most ideal scenario is raising as much money as you need until you reach profitability but, without a proven product, this is a wild guess. The more common approach is looking at raising enough funds that will keep you going until the next big milestone where you will have more leverage to raise more money with a high valuation. For example, if you are building a B2C product, after the MVP launch, your next big milestone might be 25,000 active daily users. This demonstrates product market fit with a lot of real user data to forecast future growth and product roadmap. It will also dramatically increase your valuation, as you can start using the value each user has the potential to add to the company in the form of revenue—referred to as lifetime customer value—to move your company valuation to be more science and less of an art. For a B2B product, your big milestone might be fifteen paying customers or a certain amount in sales. If you are on the right trajectory, you will be in a position to raise your next round of funding in about twelve months. That is generally the goal of a seed round, to raise enough money to be able to grow in the right trajectory for about twelve months. Also, always add a 15–20 percent buffer on top of your calculation to account for unforeseen issues.

As you go through multiple rounds, you have to understand dilution. We discussed this in a previous chapter, but let me refresh your memory, as it is important. Let's assume you do not have a cofounder and you own 100 percent of your side venture and, for ease of math, when you formed your legal entity you issued 100,000 shares or units. You raise money from family and friends and agree to issue 10,000 shares or units to them. At this point, you own 91 percent of your company, even though your number of shares is still the same, and your family and friends own 9 percent. You go through the process, do everything right, and are lucky enough to be able to raise money from an Angel investor. The Angel investor puts $300,000 in your company in exchange for 30 percent of the company. Since you have issued 110,000 shares or units and this now represents 70 percent of the company, you have to issue 47,000 new shares or units to your new Angel investor. This brings the total number of shares or units issued to 157,000. After this round of funding, you still own 100,000 shares or units, but your percentage ownership of the company is now 63.5 percent. Your family and friends still own 10,000 shares or units, but the percentage of ownership has dropped from 9 percent to 6.5 percent. This is called dilution.

Using Facebook as an example most can understand, Mark Zuckerberg now owns less than 30 percent of Facebook because of dilution, but because of the way he structured the deals, he still maintains more than 50 percent of the voting rights, allowing him to maintain control over Facebook.

Your funding goal should be to find smart money. This is an investor that can bring to the table more than just capital. Think Shark Tank investors and how they are highly sought after because of their expertise and network. Given your inexperience, the best investor will not be the one writing the largest check, but the person that understands your industry and software; can be a hands-on advisor; has a network of other investors, serial entrepreneurs, and influential people; and can guide you through both good and bad times. Most importantly, given that you still have a corporate job and this will continue being your side venture, you want to make sure your investor is fully aware of your situation and that they support it—this might result in additional rejections, but don't get discouraged. You will find the right smart investor who is willing to take a chance on you if you have all of your ducks in order.

Smart money investors are easier to close since you don't need to educate them on your industry and, based on their professional background, they can bring invaluable expertise to the table. In our case, our investor had a finance, tax, and merger and acquisition background and was able to help with cap tables and projections, help us learn accounting lingo like earnings before interest, taxes, and amortization (EBITA) and help draft agreements with employees, lawyers, partners, and other investors—not to mention helping to restructure the company from a legal standpoint for tax strategy reasons.

The drawback is that you will have to give up more of your company to smart money investors, as they also know the value they bring to the table, but you have to think long term. Owning 53 percent of a company that has value is much better than owning 75 percent of a company that has no value. The main concern is for the smart investor to not bully themselves to indirectly run the company and make day-to-day and product decisions—as long as your term sheets are clear, you will have legal grounds to not allow this to happen.

Speaking of the term sheet, you have spent months networking and talking to people, landed multiple pitch meetings, and now have a smart money investor that is ready to write a check. Do not use a template or a term sheet your accident lawyer drafts for you. Make sure you consult the right type of lawyer, as each investment is different. To protect both sides, you need a term sheet that outlines the terms of the agreement with the focus being company valuation, the amount of the investment, division of the equity, and its value on paper. The following are other items you need to cover.

Voting rights. This ties back to the type of shares being issued to the investor. For example, investors might request to have the same voting rights as the CEO, which can mean each share or unit owned equals one vote. Investors might request to have additional voting rights for specific circumstances—major hiring decisions or mergers and acquisitions before the next round of funding or big purchases. Whatever is agreed upon should be explicitly spelled out in the term sheet—such as, if you have agreed that the investor will have a board seat.

Conversion option. This means the investor has the option to convert their share type. For example, if you have preferred shares and common shares and they have slightly different voting rights and value, the investor might want the option to convert from one to the other if certain criteria are met.

Anti-dilution clause in the term sheet. There are two common types of anti-dilution clauses your investors can choose from to protect themselves: full racket and weighted average approach. These can get complex, so consult your lawyer. If you only have one investor willing to write a check, you might be in a tough position to negotiate. Just think long term and make sure a short-term decision doesn't have a negative impact on future investors unwilling to write checks. The term sheet is also used to outline the founder's obligations—your time commitment to the company and how you will contribute to the success of your venture.

Future investments. This is part of your investor's rights. For your next round of funding, your investor might require him or her to have the right of first refusal. Meaning, before you go out and raise more money, they want to be the first option to give you the full or partial amount you are trying to raise.

To conclude the term sheet, include who pays for the legal expenses to execute the term sheet and the non-disclosure agreement (NDA) as well. The last part is the signature, then congratulations. You have officially raised your first real round of funding and now it's time to get even more serious about your side venture.

Raising money is draining and oftentimes you feel defeated. It is difficult to raise money when you don't have a proven track record. Don't get discouraged until you have given it your all. If you have validated your idea, built a product based on rounds of feedback, and have early social proof, the right investor is just around the corner.

Visit the below link for a chapter summary and resources related to this chapter.

www.ch14resources.sideadventure.com

CHAPTER 15

LEADERSHIP AND TEAM MANAGEMENT

"The secret to successful hiring is this: look
for the people who want to change the world."
Marc Benioff

"The greatest leader is not necessarily the one
who does the greatest things. He is the one
that gets the people to do the greatest things."
Ronald Reagan

Building and managing an internal team where everyone is working in different locations can be challenging, especially when your side venture team might be the second team you have to manage.

This is exactly the situation I was in. With all my side venture attempts, it was either a team of one—myself—or a team of two, myself and my my cofounder, that got the idea off the ground. I would wear multiple hats for months, without the funds to be able to hire anyone. The start of the journey is both strategic and tactical and, outside of hiring a vendor for development or freelancers for design work, you can't offload the product development, strategy, and building of the company's foundation to anyone else.

Months into the process, I would start seeing the pile-up of repeatable administrative tasks and projects—I knew it was time. But again, we had no funds, so instead we would bring on an intern to work semi part-time and help out where needed. We offered flexibility, working from anywhere in the world, and the excitement of being part of a technology startup. Surprisingly, we had many students or recent grads interested, and they became our first part-time interns. We hired for potential instead of experience and looked for an individual that was resourceful, growth-minded, and was in it to learn. We wanted someone that did not require chasing to get status updates and who wanted to get their hands dirty in different areas. Of course, I sometimes made bad decisions, which led to me learning to trust my gut—if someone is not a good fit, let them go right away. Speed is the most important factor for a startup and you do not have time to waste with someone who is not a good fit.

Given the money raised for the hospitality startup, I was finally in a position to hire someone with pay. Using my values and the company culture I wanted to create, we decided that our first hire was going to be someone that had knowledge and experience in UI/UX design but also understood product development and branding, would fit into our target demographic, and had some general operational know-how—basically, more of a generalist than a specialist. Our lead investor introduced us to a candidate and fairly quickly I knew he was the best fit for us. He ended up being our best hire and he drove a lot of value for the company.

For our second hire, we wanted either a sales executive or someone that could open doors and generate leads. We had several candidates on the table but went with an internal recommendation and hired them part-time. They were able to help fill the sales pipeline and be an advisor, as they had many years of experience in the hospitality industry.

Next came marketing. After many introductions, we had a few candidates, but our investor was pushing for one specific candidate. We ended up going with this individual even though I wasn't fully sold on it but, given the large check the investor had written, I felt obligated to respect his hard recommendation. After all, we had no revenue at this point and the investor was technically paying our employees. Over a span of a year, we rounded the team with paid interns, a database developer, and back-end and front-end developers to augment the offshore vendor.

At its height, I was the leader of a team of twenty-five at my corporate job and the CEO of a startup, leading an internal team of eight at nights and weekends. We all had varying schedules living in different time zones, so it was clear that we had to nail communication methodology, otherwise this was all going to fall apart quickly. To solve this problem, we heavily relied on Slack, Jira, and Google Drive to communicate goals, the roadmap, project statuses, collaboration on presentations, and quick communication. We stayed away from email as much as possible, as the volume would have become hard to manage and stay on top of. We explored several times the idea of using a project management tool, but they all seemed overly complicated and time consuming to use for a small team.

Everyone knew that this was a side venture for me and a few others, so we were transparent with our obligations and lifestyles. To ensure we all stayed connected, we had at least three scheduled weekly team calls, which, when possible, we tried to leverage technology and have video calls instead of voice calls. Seeing people speak allowed body language and other nonverbal communication to come through—something that easily gets lost in voice calls. And once a month, on a Saturday or Sunday, we got together for an all-day meeting, which would last between eight to ten hours. It did not make sense to have permanent office space, so we became members at a WeWork type facility where we could reserve a conference room for a limited time each month.

This worked really well for us in the early days. All the Slack messages, document sharing, screen sharing, and calls from the month would come together in these in-person, immersive, and super productive sessions that would drive our focus and strategy for the following month. All our plans and projects were documented in the cloud, which allowed for easier tracking.

A few months into our marketing hire, I started noticing a bad trend: many big promises and fancy presentations but no execution and delivery. I stayed quiet, giving the person the benefit of the doubt. After a few more months, I started to lose patience and brought up my concerns with our investor. Being an amazingly nice person, he wanted to be patient and give this employee a chance—later on, he agreed that we should have let go of this person a lot sooner. I knew they were not a good fit and did not put the interest of the company first. I prioritized the interest of my relationship with our investor, which was equally important but not the right move in this instance. I should have had a candid conversation and explained that as CEO, this was my call, offered my reasoning, and asked him to trust my judgment.

In the early days of your side venture, the most valuable hires will be generalists, people who can easily wear multiple hats and enjoy it. That is why our first full-time hire was our best hire. Generalists are very resourceful, as it is a necessity to be able to jump from one area to another. This type of individual also thrives in a startup atmosphere. You want people that truly believe in your cause and what you are trying to achieve. Amazing talent that wants to be hired just because of the paycheck will not give you the same effort and passion. If you do make a mistake and hire someone that turns out to be amazing but not a believer, you have to part ways quickly.

It takes a lot of leadership to be able to manage a team effectively. Now add the dynamics of a second team in a side venture with nights and weekends as the dominant office hours and leadership becomes even more difficult. I soaked up every leadership, team management, and self-help book I could. I had a goal of one book a month and, using Kindle and Audible, I was easily hitting or exceeding my goal every month—you'll find a list of my favorite books at the resources web page mentioned at the end of this chapter. My thought process was that if the side venture didn't work out, I would become a great leader at my corporate job and build a high-performance team that was the envy of other teams. Fortunately, this did happen, on top of succeeding with the side venture as well.

The most important leadership lesson I have learned over the years is building trust with your team. For me, this starts with taking ownership and not expecting that your team members need to earn your trust. Begin by building a personal relationship and being genuinely interested in them as individuals. Once the seeds of the relationships have been planted, it becomes easier to communicate your goals and vision. Then give the person freedom and empower them to solve the problem and complete a task on their own terms while keeping your goal, vision, and timeline in mind. Not only does this demonstrate your trust, but it also allows you to quickly see the individual's productivity and work ethic.

Just as important as building trust is leading by example. As the founder of a startup that is not generating profit—you have to wear many hats and excel at everything you do, which will demonstrate to the team that you expect nothing less than excellence from them as well.

Always begin by looking in the mirror before reacting externally toward a team member. The name of the game is failing fast until you succeed. What this really means is that it is rare for your original idea to manifest as-is into a product to find product market fit. Through failures and iterations is how you arrive at product market fit, so failing and freely talking about the failures should be part of your culture. You want many small failures, so big mistakes do not happen when they count. When these small failures do happen, ask yourself: As a leader, what could I have done to support the team better? Did I communicate my expectations clearly? Was my direction flawed? By starting inward first, before focusing on the team, you are accelerating your own leadership development by being more self-aware.

When you switch to look at the individual's performance, use it as a growth opportunity for them as well, but act quickly if an individual is not a good fit. Decisive action for underperformance is making a statement that you expect nothing but excellence. Your goal with the initial hires is to build future leaders, assuming you will be successful and go all in to scale the company. This will only happen if you have a growth mindset yourself and inject this mindset into everyone else by way of your culture. With the right foundation and a great product, leaders can help your company grow exponentially instead of having linear sales and user growth with average hires in the early stages.

Avoid establishing a fear-based culture. This is true for all organizations but especially true for startups, as speed is critical. The more frequent feedback you get from customers and users, the faster you know if something will work or not. The same is true internally. You want everyone to be able to share ideas openly and speak up when there are issues or if they feel a bad decision was made. A fear-based culture doesn't allow for this to happen. Instead, everyone is agreeing with the leader when face to face, and once in smaller groups all the chatter and gossip happens behind the leader's back. This is toxic for the culture, which can have a detrimental impact on the side venture. You want everyone focused on the same vision and executing instead of wasting time on politics.

These are all soft skills you need to work on, and no matter what path your career takes, you will benefit from developing soft leadership skills. There are some practical things you can also do to be efficient as a remote team, similar to the team I had for my side ventures.

Establishing communication guidelines and SLAs is by far the most important, and you have to take the lead to establish them. Everyone must be on the same chat tools and use it with agreed-upon rules. For example, Slack is a great tool, but unless you have some rules around its usage, it can get messy very quickly.

Establish the cadence of weekly team video or voice conference calls. Given that you and others might have other jobs during the day, block out one hour after 6 p.m., two times a week, and one meeting over the weekends, and get everyone to agree to the commitment and set expectations that since everyone has agreed to having a certain number of standing calls during the week that they must be present—unless a valid reason is given. Don't use lack of time as a reason to not have one-on-one meetings with team members. They can be one thirty-minute meeting a month at the minimum. This will allow you to hear issues the individual wants to raise with you. It also allows the person to feel important and part of the team instead of one of many. Everyone is working odd hours and putting in a lot of effort for below-market pay, as you don't have the budget, so you want to get a chance to thank them individually and keep them engaged.

Beyond communication tools, establish and use tools to simplify processes to save time. For example, ad hoc meetings with part of the team or a specific individual will need to be scheduled as things come up. Do not rely on email back and forth to figure out availability, as it can waste a lot of time, especially when at the very least you are mostly limited to early mornings, evenings, and weekends—I use Calendly, but there are many tools in the market for this use. Agree on a tool to manage documents, projects, and brainstorming sessions. Passing back and forth Excel and Word docs is not efficient. We decided on Good Drive, but something else might work better for you and your team.

Get the entire team together at least once a month. There is no substitute for the energy created when everyone is physically together working on the same problem. This is how cultures are built and strengthened. This is how you truly see the character of each person. Working remotely might feel convenient and it definitely works for certain tasks, projects, and communication, but it is not a replacement for team building, comradery, and when trying to build a culture from the ground up. Without regular immersive collaboration, like we were doing once a month, team members might start to feel like consultants.

With a great team that knows how to work with each other remotely and has the seeds of a great culture, you can pivot successfully several times until you find product market fit, but with a team that's lacking cohesiveness, effective communication, and belief, the most groundbreaking idea will hit a wall. Once you are ready to hire a team, spend time identifying the right talent and establishing the rules of engagement.

Visit the below link for a chapter summary and resources related to this chapter.

www.ch15resources.sideadventure.com

CHAPTER 16

WHAT IS ALL THIS FOR?

"Your work is going to fill a large part of your
life, and the only way to be truly satisfied is
to do what you believe is great work. And the
only way to do great work is to love what you
do." Steve Jobs

"I knew that if I failed I wouldn't regret that,
but I knew the one thing I might regret is not
trying." Jeff Bezos

I started writing this book about six months before my son was
born, and as I write this chapter, he is twenty months old. I
was out of being involved in the day-to-day of the hospitality
company, as acquisition conversations had been in progress for
a while and I had begun thinking about my next side venture.
My gut feeling was telling me that juggling being a dad for the
first time while also being an executive in a media company and
writing a book was going to be hard to manage.

The new side venture had given me new motivation and
excitement, as, yet again, I was tackling a problem I deeply
understood and cared about and had a very good name for it.
I named the product Effishient and told myself I'd take it slow
on the book to try to push for six months to build a fully self-
funded MVP before my son was born. Things didn't work out

as planned. As is typical with all startups, there were delays, so I was around 40 percent into building the MVP when my son was born.

As far as the book, I had a framework, outline, and a lot of notes and maybe part of the first chapter completed, but I had realized that I was really enjoying the process, even though it was moving forward slowly. At the same time, the media company I worked for made two big announcements: they were launching their own streaming service and they had made an offer to purchase another major media company. This also presented potential career advancement opportunities, as I was thinking about making the best decision for my family, one that would also allow me to be the hands-on father I wanted to be.

As a result, I put the book and the new side venture on pause to focus on finding my footing on being a great dad while understanding how I was going to add value to the huge investments the company I worked for was making. It took months, but eventually I figured out how to manage my schedule. I was enjoying being a dad. Meanwhile, an opportunity presented itself to play a big role in both the new streaming service and the integration of the new acquisition. These had the potential to lead to personal career advancement in the corporate world.

But the voice in the back of my mind never went away. It kept telling me I was capable of so much more. The voice kept asking me: When you are ninety-five and on your deathbed, what are you going to be most proud of? The answer was clear: I'm going to be proud of the father and husband I was and how I was able to help others. I'm going to be proud of the positive legacy I'm leaving behind instead of just being a statistic.

The thought of wanting to be rich as the measure of being successful never crossed my mind. I didn't even think about being successful. I was thinking about how I could be valuable to my family and others. But a funny thing happens when you focus on being valuable. Success and money follow.

With this mindset, I told myself that I needed to turn up the heat on being valuable for the company I was working for and help drive the two major projects I was working on until completion. For the immediate future, that was the best option for my family, as it allowed me to be a hands-on dad. I continued to write the book, as it became my side venture and directly aligned with my purpose, while making sure family was my priority. Because I was so deep into Effishient, I just couldn't quit, so it became a background project. Instead of my initial goal of an MVP in six months, I completed the MVP in twenty months just to say I completed it.

Around the same time, my wife and I found out she was pregnant with our daughter, so now I had another hard deadline. Both my son and my daughter were IVF pregnancies. We went through many disappointments and heartache until my wife was pregnant with our son, so the last and final attempt for a second pregnancy was not something I had high hopes for, but we stayed positive and it worked. I think we were both surprised and extremely grateful. I can also say that I am now a semi-professional when it comes to the IVF process from a father's perspective and I think I'm better than most nurses when it comes to giving shots.

Since I had not worked on my go-to-market strategy for Effishient, I decided to put it on pause and focus on the completion of this book. I knew writing this book was going to take a very long time, so I programmed myself to look at this as another side venture, one that is more like a marathon instead of a 100-meter dash. I also wanted to be able to tell my son and daughter that, while raising them, I was in the middle of getting the hospitality company acquired, working on another side venture, progressing my career in the corporate world, and writing a book—if I can do all of this, there is nothing they can't do. I wanted to apply my leadership skills to be a great dad and lead by example.

Then in late January of 2020, the basketball world, if not the entire world, was hit with the tragedy of Kobe Bryant's death. I grew up in Los Angeles and, as a die-hard Lakers fan, I was heartbroken. I did not want to believe it. Being around the same age as Kobe Bryant, I felt like I grew up with him. I even made my own tribute video—which I will share with you at the end of this chapter. The tragedy made me realize what's truly important in life. Here is one of the greatest basketball players of all time with all the accolades and achievements, but what dominated the storylines was what an amazing father he was to his daughters—he called himself a "girl dad."

This got me even more excited that I was going to be a girl dad and validated my letting go of the hospitality company and putting family first. I would not be here writing this book without the experience, knowledge, success, and failures of the hospitality company and all other side venture attempts that came before it. I was single, working long nights, traveling around from one pitch to another, and got others to follow me in that adventure. It was my main focus, but after I got married and became a parent, I knew it would be hard to keep things going in the same way, unless I either went all in or got out because of an acquisition. So, when the possibility of an acquisition came up, I strongly voted for it.

Shortly after, the hard work I had put in for about a year to be valuable in my corporate job paid off, and a career advancement opportunity was presented to me. Weeks later, the world was shocked by the new Coronavirus, the stock market began sinking, and millions of people got either laid off or furloughed in the United States alone. Some experts predicted the worst economic fallout since the Great Depression in 1929.

It is ironic that in the last chapter I talked about managing a remote team while the pandemic forced half of the working population to work from home and hundreds, if not thousands, of articles and videos popped up around best practices in managing remote teams and working remotely. I wrote the first draft of every chapter before this chapter at a local Starbucks or somewhere away from home where I could focus and not get distracted by things that have to be done around the house or helping my wife with a baby who grew into a toddler during this time. This usually meant nights after our son was sleeping, during his nap times over the weekends, or when my wife was out with him and I was by myself. Unlike the side venture, writing the book in the mornings was out of the question, as my son got my side of the genes and is an early bird. Mornings are our favorite bonding time.

Meanwhile, I've been focused on showing value in my new elevated executive role and Effishient is on pause. You might be wondering why I'm providing you with this backstory now. I wanted to make sure you had either started your adventure or had a much better understanding of what it took to pursue a side venture before telling you what was happening in my life during and toward the end of writing this book.

The true goal of this book is not to push you to become an entrepreneur and start your own business. It is to help you figure out what makes you happy as soon as possible so you can focus on that instead of wondering, coming up with one idea after another without knowing how to pursue it, and being on your deathbed with major regrets that you did not give an idea a chance.

During your adventure, you might realize that you love the entrepreneurial process. You love being involved in all aspects of building a product and a company, the uncertainty, hard work, failures, challenges, victories, and the close bond you build with a small group of people that bring your idea to life. You might figure out that you like aspects of the process but not the entire process. This can lead you to work for a company that allows you to be an intrapreneur (someone who feels like an entrepreneur but under the safety of a larger company, where they don't have to worry about resources and other challenges that come when building a company from the ground up) instead of the job you have now. Or you decide that the idea of being an entrepreneur sounded good but in actuality, it's not for you, as you prefer stability and a structured working environment.

There is no right or wrong answer. We are all individuals and have the right to happiness, but you have to give things a try before really knowing what happiness means to you. It all comes down to realizing that everything you do is because you are chasing a specific type of feeling instead of material objects or money. You don't desire the fancy car just because. You desire the fancy car because it makes you feel a certain way.

If you do the math, most people give over one hundred thousand hours to work. This is probably an underestimate for the workaholics like myself where we rarely get close to a forty-hour workweek. That is a lot of time spent working, so you should not settle for working at a place or for someone that makes you miserable. If entrepreneurship is what makes you happy, use the person or organization that is making you miserable as motivation to drive your side venture forward to someday become a true full-time entrepreneur. But don't just quit your job unless you have some other means of being financially stable. Research does show that starting your side venture while keeping your day job leads to a higher chance of success. It also gives you an avenue to be fulfilled, so a horrible boss or boring job doesn't dominate your thoughts all day. Before you decide to play your fantasy of walking into your boss's office and telling them you quit, why you're quitting, and everything they have been doing wrong, make sure the below is in place.

Your side venture needs to be generating enough revenue so you can start taking as little salary as possible to cover your living expenses. Because you have already worked on your finances, you should know what this number is. In addition, you should have six months of savings to cover you in case there is a decrease in revenue and you need to reduce your salary.

As part of your finances, you need to account for yours and, if applicable, your family's health insurance. You won't have a company contributing towards your health insurance, so you need to make sure you and your family are covered. Going into debt for a health issue without adequate care can have an adverse impact on your venture.

The revenue forecast should be going up. You should be able to tell this by your sales pipeline and conversion rates.

If your side venture is a B2C product that is not at the revenue stage yet but adoption is growing exponentially, then as part of your fundraising negotiations you need to make sure you guarantee yourself two years of salary to cover yourself in case things don't go as planned.

Don't forget about retirement planning. If you were contributing to a 401K, make sure you can continue doing so. If you were putting money into a college plan, make sure you continue to do so. You do not want to put your family under any financial stress.

Speaking of your family, if you are married, you need to make sure your family is part of the decision process to quit or not quit. Listen and don't get defensive if they react in a way you were not expecting. Let them explain their position, which in most cases will be tied to their stability. It will be your job to show them you have thought about everything mentioned above and that they do not need to worry about the financial health of the family. In reverse, you need to be open about changing your mind.

If you have checked off all of the above, you can now quit your job—do so with grace, appreciation, and gratitude, because the job you're quitting allowed you to fund your side venture. If you had a horrible boss, they were part of the motivation to pursue your side venture, so thank them instead. Most importantly, you do not want to burn any bridges. Life can throw things at you that you did not expect and you might need the help of your network in the future—the COVID-19 pandemic is an extreme but real example of a curveball that can completely alter your plans.

If as part of pursuing your side venture you have realized that the concept of being an entrepreneur was much better than being one but you now know exactly the type of role and work that makes you happy, go pursue that. Maybe you want a stable role that is predictable or a role that allows you to be an intrapreneur. The good part is that you now know, so go after what you want.

The other outcome is that your side venture has failed, but you loved the process and are hungrier and more motivated than before. Or life circumstances are leading you in a different direction for the time being. This is OK. It doesn't mean things will stay the same and you can't pursue a side venture in the future. The failure was a learning experience that makes you better. Because I did not have a go-to-market strategy for Effishient, even though the MVP was great, at the moment I classify it as a failure. With a twenty-month-old son that I adore who I cannot wait to hear say "Hi dada" every morning, a newborn daughter, an unbelievably supportive wife, and being offered a senior executive role where I can be an intrapreneur and do the type of work I love while having an amazing boss, being in the middle of a pandemic where millions are losing their jobs, and finding funding for Effishient or a new side venture more difficult than ever, the decisions I have made were in the best interest of my family and one that I'm happy about. But I still had to find another outlet to be creative on my own terms. This book became that vehicle for me without having to sacrifice time with my son and family. On top of that, it allows me to share my knowledge and experience with you to help you discover who you are and what makes you happy, the same way I did.

I am nowhere close to being done and I know I'm one idea away from a side venture that I would like to turn into much bigger successes than the hospitality company. I know without a doubt that you are also one idea away from your happiness. The adventure I have been on thus far has kept me happy, and when the time comes to answer the question "What are you most proud of?" I can say with certainty, I'm proud of the father and husband I've been, I'm proud of helping people go through their own journey to find happiness, and I was truly happy most of the time with the work I did. At the end of the day, isn't this what life is all about?

CPSIA information can be obtained
at www.ICGtesting.com
Printed in the USA
FSHW021552240321
79754FS